HIRE TOUGH,
MANAGE EASY

How to Find and Hire the Best Hourly Employees

Mel Kleiman

Published
by

Houston, Texas

PRINTING HISTORY
1st printing – January 1999
2nd printing – October 1999

Published by HTG Press a division of
Humetrics, Inc.
8300 Bissonnet, Suite 490
Houston, TX 77074
http://www.humetrics.com
http://www.hiretough.com

Printed in the United States of America

Library of Congress Catalog Card Number 98-89967
ISBN 1-893214-00-1

In memory of Sarah C. Kleiman.
Mom would have been proud.

Acknowledgments

Without the help of Leslie Hamel this book would have remained a work-in-progress. Her writing, editing, and typesetting skills, as well as her persistence are what made it a reality.

Many people have contributed to these pages by providing content, ideas, and critiques of various manuscript drafts. Without their hard work and dedication this book would not have been possible. Individuals who deserve recognition are (in alphabetical order): Paula Aguirre, Wendy Clark, Christine Hebel, Heather Killough, Andy Mastroianni, and Diane Slavin.

And special thanks to Cathy Schmermund for helping us translate the spoken word into the written word, Roni Richards for helping bring together the various pieces, and Baxter+Korge for the cover design.

Thanks are also due to Humetrics' and the Hire Tough Group's clients. Without our partnership over the past 25 years, these ideas could never have been tested and proved in the real world.

Finally, to my family – Roberta, Brent, Steven, Robyn, Debi, and especially my father, Sam – thanks for your support and for encouraging me to write this book instead of just talk about it.

Foreword

If there were only one recommendation I could make to every leader in every organization today, it would be to follow Mel Kleiman's advice to "Hire Tough, Manage Easy."

Having worked with "best in class" organizations throughout the world for the last 25 years, I've noted some characteristics and practices these exemplary firms have in common. One of their "secrets" is the significance their leaders place on employee selection. They clearly understand the importance of hiring people who have "walk in" positive attitudes and who fit their cultures. They also know attempting to fix "people problems" after someone is hired is, at best, a poor use of time and talent and, at worst, full of costly consequences and a drain on valuable resources. They recognize hiring is a "front-end" loaded situation – not a "back-end" issue to deal with later. Bottom line, they leverage success by using the power of hiring tough in order to manage easy.

This book drives home the importance of the "hire tough" approach and gives us practical tools for accomplishing this objective. Everyone who uses this powerful resource will avoid the pitfalls of poor hiring decisions, and gain the skills and confidence needed to select the best and brightest from the available applicant pool.

I highly recommend this resource to everyone who has a stake in good hiring decisions – from the newest supervisor to the most seasoned professional. I know I'm going to keep "Hire Tough, Manage Easy" within reach and use it on a regular basis!

Eric L. Harvey, President
The WALK THE TALK® Company

Contents

Recruiting *(cont.)*

Selection Systems

Selection System Tools

Selection System Tools *(cont.)*

Selection System Benefits

The Interview

The Interview *(cont.)*

Introduction

> **"If you hire the wrong people, all the fancy management techniques in the world won't bail you out."**
> – *Red Auerbach, president of the Boston Celtics*

While I love Red's quote, I once heard someone say it even better.

About ten years ago, at one of my seminars, I couldn't help but notice a man in the front row, furiously taking pages of notes. I figured he must be new to supervising or managing because he was so keenly interested in every word I was saying. So, when I found out he actually had built a small empire comprised of 14 different businesses, I just had to ask why he was so extraordinarily attentive.

"I only have one job," he told me, "and that is to hire the right people. If I hire the right people, I don't have to do anything else. The most important decisions I make are hiring decisions."

Just ask Siva Tayi, president of Houston-based Sai Software Consultants and winner of a 1997 Entrepreneur of the Year Award. He'll tell you how one employee – the first he ever hired – single-handedly determined the success of his company.

Shortly after he started his computer software and consulting business in 1984, Tayi's secretary – and only employee – answered a phone call from a natural gas company inquiring about Sai's ability to work on a linear programming project. Without hesitation, she told the caller she would transfer him to the Linear Programming

Department. Then she put the call on hold and alerted her boss.

The rest, as they say, is history. Today, the company has 425 employees, ten offices nationwide, annual sales of $30 million, and is on track to become a $100 million company by 2000. And all because an employee was smart, caring, and resourceful enough to say, "Let me connect you with our Linear Programming Department."

People make the difference. These days, the only difference between you and your competition is the people you hire. You can have a great restaurant, in a prime location, and competitive prices, but if your employees deliver lackluster service, you'll be out of business in six months. Yet, if you have a great restaurant, in an out-of-the-way place, staffed by employees who know how to please customers, people will flock to it.

Whether it's the convenience store, grocery, hotel, hospitality, restaurant, healthcare, computer, or oil-and-gas industry, quality products and great customer service start with employees. The success of every business hinges on its ability to recruit, select, and hire winners.

The bad news is most business people put more thought and care into writing big-ticket purchase orders than they do to hiring new employees. How much research do you do and how much justifying documentation do you write before requesting a $5,000 piece of office equipment? Did you ever stop to think about the cost of a new employee? The minimum a full-time person is going to cost is at least $900 a month – that's $10,800 a year. Do you spend as much time and effort deciding who to hire – a choice that's going to cost you more money and have a more dramatic effect on the bottom line?

Unfortunately, most hiring decisions usually aren't good enough. According to the U.S. Department of Labor, about half of the hourly employees hired are gone within six months. That's 100 percent turnover per year. And the total spent on hiring just hourly employees in 1996 was estimated at $26 billion.

Instead of spending your time and money doing it over and over again, why not hire right the first time? That's what this book is about. It provides practical advice and proven techniques that will help you do a better job of hiring the right people – the first time.

When it comes to hiring hourly workers, hiring right is particularly important. These are the employees who determine the success of most business enterprises. They represent 79 percent of the U.S. labor force and hold the front-line positions – those closest to customers. If the president of a fast food franchise doesn't show up for work, how many customers will notice? But if the restroom doesn't get cleaned or the wrong food order is delivered, will the customer return? Not likely.

The information in this book is based on more than 20 years of experience hiring and influencing the hiring of thousands of people, designing recruiting and selection systems for clients nationwide, and speaking engagements for hundreds of trade or professional associations and individual corporations.

If you have never interviewed or hired before, this book covers the tools, procedures, and systems needed to do the best job possible. If you have a lot of experience, this book provides some unique ideas and approaches that will save you time, energy, and money.

The Challenges

Change

*The rapid pace of change
is creating a new world.*

While change has long been the only permanent fea-
ture of the American workplace, consider what's happened lately:

- **Companies are changing.** Downsizing, up-
  sizing, resizing, rightsizing, and reengineer-
  ing are changing the way companies work.
- **Technology is changing.** In some cases, it's
  making jobs more complex. In other cases,
  it's making them essentially dummy-proof.
- **Competition is changing.** Look at what Federal Express and UPS have done to the U.S.
  Postal Service. Restaurants, grocery stores,
  and convenience stores compete today not
  only within their own category, but with each
  other. Since 1995, Americans have been
  spending more money on food purchased at
  restaurants than on food bought at grocery
  stores.
- **People are changing.** Increasing diversity in
  our population will continue to expand our
  beliefs, values, and experiences.

As a result, all jobs are changing.

And consider how quickly things change:

- About 70 percent of all products on grocery shelves today are either new or in different packages than they were five years ago.
- In just 10 years, the cellular phone industry grew from zero to 24 million subscribers.
- About 1,700 new products were introduced in grocery dairy cases during 1997.
- In 1990, it took Ford, GM and Chrysler six years to develop a new car. Now they do it in two years or less.
- Over 80 percent of Miller Brewing's revenue comes from products that have been changed significantly or didn't even exist within the past 24 months.
- More than half of Hewlett Packard's revenue comes from products that didn't even exist one year ago.

The challenge facing today's managers is figuring out how to capitalize on these changes and hire the right people – the people who will make their organizations winners in the years to come.

The Challenges

Labor Market

*There will always be enough employees,
but never enough good ones.*

There are more jobs now – 121.8 million – than ever before. In some cases, we're even experiencing negative unemployment – there are more job openings than there are qualified people to fill them. The restaurant industry alone expects to create four million new jobs in the next five years.

In this environment, finding employees – much less the competent, motivated, productive people businesses need to be successful – is becoming increasingly difficult:

- Two months after a new restaurant was built, it finally opened. It took that long to staff it.
- In Minneapolis, where there's 1.3 percent unemployment, a convenience-store operator ran a help-wanted ad for four consecutive Sundays and received no applicants.

Even when unemployment levels are normal or high, hiring is a challenge. There may be a tremendous flow of applicants, but it's still difficult to identify the best ones. Without the appropriate skills and tools, it's nearly impossible to tell the eagles from the turkeys.

It's long past time to change the mindset that employees are easy to find and can be easily replaced. In today's world, the old ways of staffing no longer work.

The Challenges

Scary Hiring

*Desperate times don't call
for desperate acts.*

Some desperate managers are taking drastic measures in order to find the workers they need:

- In its ad for warehouse people, a North Carolina company stated, "No drug testing."
- Through random testing, another company discovered that 20 employees were using drugs. The employees weren't fired because the company knew it wouldn't be able to find new people to replace them.
- Many managers are overworking their best employees to the point of burnout.
- Not bothering to interview applicants and not checking references are acts of desperation.

No matter what form the desperation takes, the result is the same. You end up hiring problem employees – the ones you spend all your time managing, eventually firing, and replacing. The challenge is finding ways to hire the right people in a tight labor market without lowering job requirements or your standards.

The Challenges

Turnover

*Low-cost employees aren't low-cost
at all if they quit in three months.*

There are all kinds of statistics on what it costs to hire a new employee. At the hourly level, costs can be anywhere from $300 to $5,000 for recruitment advertising, processing, and background checks, etc.

But there's more to it than just hiring costs. You also have to consider the cost of turnover. These costs are related to the training and managerial time needed to bring a new employee up to speed. While positions are vacant or filled by trainees, losses in productivity, efficiency, and sales are tremendous.

A roof truss company we work with knows exactly what its costs are for hourly employee turnover:

On any given day, a good, three-man team can build $7,500 worth of trusses. If one of these $6-per-hour employees leaves and the company has to bring in somebody new, production drops by 20 percent for at least the first week. That's $1,500 a day – or $7,500 a week – in just the first week. It takes up to four weeks for the team to get back up to full productivity. So, losing a $6-per-hour person costs this company somewhere between $15,000 and $20,000 over four weeks.

To figure out your total turnover costs, you have to know what your real turnover is. Most people simply look at the total number of people on staff versus the number hired in a year, but that number doesn't necessarily tell the whole story. While you may calculate you have 20 percent turnover, in reality, three jobs out of 100 turned seven times during the year. This suggests there's a much more serious turnover problem than the overall figure indicates. So, a better use of turnover data is to determine what's happening where. Then you can investigate the reason behind it – a particular job, location, manager, or supervisor – and decide if and how to resolve the problem.

My favorite definition of insanity is: "Doing the same things over and over again, expecting a different result." Most U.S. companies use this "insane" approach when hiring. The resulting turnover is an unnecessary drain on productivity and profitability.

The Challenges

Hiring Costs

The most expensive person you'll ever hire is the one you have to fire.

- Recruiting, screening, interviewing, hiring, and training a new employee costs between 300 and 700 times that person's hourly wage.

- There's increased legal exposure every time an organization hires. Research indicates that 70 percent of all workers' compensation claims are made in an employee's first 60 to 90 days on the job.

- Hiring an employee with the wrong attitude can have a significant impact on customer loyalty. According to an often quoted study, 68 percent of customers who stop associating with a business do so because of an employee's indifference toward the customer.

No business can afford to lose customers. About 65 percent of most business comes from present customers and it costs five times more to get a new customer than to keep a current one.

The impact also spreads to other existing and potential customers as more than nine out of 10 unsatisfied customers will tell at least nine other people about their bad experience.

- Poor hiring decisions are also costly in terms of lost profits, missed opportunities, decreased productivity, increased stress, and lower employee morale. The wrong decision can jeopardize your company's assets, its reputation, and your job security.

- The costs are even greater when an employee isn't replaced immediately. When other employees have to work longer hours to get the job done, it costs you overtime. And if employees get frustrated with prolonged extra duty demands, they'll quit and increase your turnover even more.

With the cost of turnover so high, can you afford to keep hiring the wrong people – again and again and again?

The Challenges

The Good Side of Turnover

The goal is not to eliminate turnover, but to manage it.

Not all turnover is bad. Without turnover, a company and its people stagnate. The challenge is determining where and what level of turnover will ensure consistency, while also promoting growth and change.

When turnover is managed, hiring becomes an opportunity instead of a headache. Every time you hire, it's a chance to improve the organization by hiring people with different or better abilities and qualities, to increase diversity and to restructure jobs to accommodate changes. Every time you hire, not only do new employees start with a clean slate, you do too. Look at each new hire as an opportunity to create a new and better organization.

The good side of turnover is also evident when someone you'd like to see leave quits. You're glad the person is gone and all your exceptional employees say, "Thank goodness."

The Challenges

Return-on-Investment

***Hiring is only costly when
it's not done well.***

Most employers only give lip service to the concept of treating their employees as their "most important asset." Yet, when hiring is done well, it's an investment. You have the right people in the right jobs, doing their best to help your organization succeed.

Just as we talk about the lifetime value of a customer, consider the lifetime value of a good employee. Surveys continually show that companies with higher employee retention rates also enjoy higher customer retention rates.

The Best Employees

Turkeys & Eagles

*It's tough to find the eagles
in a flock of turkeys.*

One of the reasons it's so hard to find the best employees is because there are so many turkeys out there. We've all hired a few. Not intentionally, of course. During the hiring process, we certainly thought they were eagles. But somehow, between the time we interviewed them and the time they showed up for work, they turned into turkeys:

- An applicant for a bank teller's position impressed management at three different interviews with her professional appearance. On her first day of work, however, she showed up dressed like a rock 'n roll groupie. When asked about the wardrobe change, she confessed she had borrowed the business suits from a friend just for interviews.

- A cashier, fired for stealing, went down the street and applied at another store, and even had the gumption to list his previous employer as a reference. Of course, the applicant seemed to be a strong candidate – he had all that experience under his belt. Good thing the potential employer always made it a point to check references.

- A college student went home for the summer
  to look for a job as a waiter. The first two
  restaurants he applied at turned him down
  because they didn't want to spend time
  training someone who would leave to go
  back to school in just three months. When
  the third restaurant asked where he was at-
  tending college, he gave the name of the local community college where he was taking
  three credit hours of summer school. He was
  hired. Can you guess what happened come
  mid-August? This turkey quit to go back to
  school.

The Best Employees

Turkeys & Eagles

*All the turkeys have learned how
to dress up to look like eagles.*

Of course, the real problem isn't that eagles suddenly change into turkeys. It's that the turkeys are so good at disguising themselves as eagles. They figure out what the employer wants and they provide it – they know how to look, act, and sound like eagles:

- They have a good answer for every question.
- They tell us what we want to hear - not what we need to know.
- They do whatever it takes to get the job.
- They're better at interviewing than the interviewers are.

How did they get so good at interviewing? For one thing, they get lots of practice. For another, they have plenty of help. Hundreds of self-help and career-development books are geared toward helping applicants become experts at getting jobs. A recent bestseller on college campuses was *Knock 'Em Dead*, a collection of the 200 toughest interview questions – with pat answers provided!

There are ways, however, to avoid being dazzled by applicants' all-purpose, pat answers. The more we know about what we really need, the less likely it is we'll be fooled by turkeys dressed up to look like eagles.

The Best Employees

Turkeys & Eagles

***Eagles don't always
look like eagles.***

The same goes for eagles; we don't always recognize them either. We could have the best waiter, clerk, or truck driver in the world applying for a job, but for one reason or another, we don't like what we see or hear because the person doesn't fit our image of "the best."

Most people make a hire/don't hire decision within the first 30 seconds of meeting an applicant. These snap decisions are based on something about the person that reminds them of things they like or don't like. In today's marketplace, however, we can't afford to let personal bias and prejudice get in the way. Times are changing; eagles won't always "look" like we think they should:

- In the past 20 years, 66 percent of all new jobs were filled by women.
- English is the second language of 55 percent of the workforce in the Southwest U.S. (Texas, Arizona, New Mexico, California).
- The Asian and Hispanic populations are growing five times faster than the rest of the population.
- By 2000, only 12 percent of new job applicants will be white males.
- By 2001, the median age of the U.S. population will increase to 37.

- By 2005:
  1. Twenty-two percent of new workers will be immigrants.
  2. Sixty-two percent of the workforce and 72 percent of new applicants will be female or minorities.

The Best Employees

Turkeys & Eagles

The government has taken all the turkeys and put them on the endangered species list.

When the eagle we thought we hired turns out to be a turkey, we figure it's a training problem. When training doesn't work, we think it's a motivation problem. But after a lot of time and effort, things still don't improve much. We just end up with a trained, motivated turkey. If we decide to fire the turkey, we discover it's a risky and potentially expensive proposition:

- Terminated turkeys are increasingly likely to file lawsuits – and win. Labor law says you're guilty until you can prove you're innocent.

- Termination cases represent the single fastest-growing area of business-related lawsuits today. And the stakes are high. The average amount awarded to employees who file and win such suits in 1995 was $204,310.

- It's costly even if the company is found "not guilty." The average cost of defending against a termination lawsuit is between $80,000 and $100,000 and that's just legal fees. Add to that all the time, effort, and energy the organization spends defending itself.

- Even when a lawsuit isn't filed, there's money involved. The employee may file for unemployment and you may pay severance, accrued vacation, or other employee-benefit amounts.

When Disney fired its second-in-command, it cost the company $90 million. When AT&T fired an executive after only nine months on the job, it cost $25.8 million. While these amounts are extreme, even if the price tag on employee termination is only $900 or $1,000, can you afford to make that kind of mistake over and over again?

The only sure defense is a strong offense. Don't hire the problem in the first place.

The Best Employees

Job Description

Looking for an employee without knowing exactly what you need is like grocery shopping without a list.

The main reason we don't have the best employees – and why we get fooled by the turkeys – is that we don't know what the best looks like.

It's just like grocery shopping. The most important thing you need when you go to the grocery store is your list. Without a list:

- You don't get everything you need.
- You get things you really don't need.
- You spend more money than you planned.
- You spend more time than your planned.
- You have to go back and do it again.

Shopping for an employee is also easier and more efficient when you have a list. To avoid getting more or less than you need and wasting time and money on unqualified applicants, you need a list of the key attributes the ideal jobholder will possess. Once you know what you need, you can figure out where and how to get it.

An employee "shopping list" also serves as a legal document. A written job description that lists the mental and physical capacities required and why the job exists is the best defense against claims of discrimination under the Americans with Disabilities Act.

A written description of what a job requires also entitles you to ask applicants if they can do specific tasks the job requires. If there are any tasks an applicant can't perform, the Americans with Disabilities Act requires you to ask for the person's suggestions on how the job could be restructured or modified (the accommodations they might recommend) so that he or she could do it. Whatever is suggested must be considered and refused only if it would create an unreasonable burden or hardship for the employer.

And as long as you do it in a non-discriminatory manner – meaning you ask everyone, not just certain people – you can also ask applicants to show you how they would perform the tasks. (If there's any chance of physical injury, be sure to have the applicant sign a waiver beforehand.)

Applicants' responses to these two inquiries – describing how they would and demonstrating they can do the task – go a long way toward helping you identify qualified candidates.

The Best Employees

Job Analysis

*The job description is a snapshot;
a job analysis is a motion picture.*

In the employment world, the shopping list is technically known as a job description.

It documents the essential elements required to do the job. Even better than a job description is a job analysis. Designed for real – versus government – use, this document directly reflects the job today and its potential for the future:

- Start by considering the reasons the job exists. (Why it's essential to the company and what you're trying to accomplish through this job.)
- Then, define the objectives of the job and the responsibilities of the jobholder:
    1. What the jobholder must do well to earn a raise.
    2. Why you would reprimand or fire a person in this job.
    3. What the last jobholder did well and not so well.
    4. What you'd like to see done differently.
    5. What has kept jobholders from being successful in the past.
    6. What you want to make sure nobody in this job ever does again.

- Make the analysis not only job specific, but location and shift specific. Different conditions and situations require different qualities and abilities.
- Make sure you focus on real criteria versus wishes or preferences. The goal – for shopping and legal purposes – is determining the essential job functions and critical requirements.
- Explore all avenues. Don't assume the way a job is being done now is the only way it can be done.
- Get input and opinions from employees, supervisors, and others who interface with the position.
- Once created, the job analysis needs to be revisited every time you need to hire for that position. Review it to ensure it's up-to-date and reflects any technological, environmental, structural, or managerial changes that have occurred or are anticipated.

The result will be a detailed profile of the qualities and abilities best suited for the job.

The Best Employees

Job Analysis

Hiring may not be the answer.

In most cases, employers look at hiring because someone left a position or growth dictates an increase in the number of positions. There's always a possibility, however, you may not really need to go out and hire. In conducting the job analysis, you may discover you can eliminate the job or restructure it.

- **Hiring Alternatives.** There may be others who can do this job. Assigning all or parts of it to existing employees, using temporary employees, or job sharing are some alternatives to hiring a permanent, full-time worker.

- **Automate.** Has technology changed what's needed? Word processing, for example, has eliminated many typist and secretarial positions; accounting software has replaced accountants; scanners at grocery stores have eliminated the need for cashiers to know prices; pay-at-the-pump has reduced the number of attendants needed at gas stations.

- **Business Changes.** Jobs can be redesigned or eliminated by changing the business process involved.

For example:

1. Many fast-food restaurants now have self-serve beverages. It's cheaper to offer free refills than to hire the extra help required to operate beverage dispensers behind the counter.

2. In a Taco Bell test program, the terminals were turned around for customers to enter their own orders. It worked great, but the concept was a little ahead of its time. Until electronic payments are possible and popular, employees are still needed to process cash transactions.

3. A number of convenience stores have stopped selling lottery tickets because the costs of staffing, theft, and the breakdown in customer service on big jackpot days aren't justified by the income per ticket.

The Best Employees

Job Analysis

*A job analysis profiles a
job in terms of C.A.P.S.*

The easiest way to write a job analysis and create
your shopping list is to think of a job's objectives and requirements as generally falling into four primary categories:

- **Capacity.** The mental and physical proficien-
  cies required to do the job.
- **Attitudes.** Dispositions needed for success,
  such as dependability, initiative, and customer service orientation.
- **Personality.** Temperament that best fits the
  job and organization, traits such as competitiveness, assertiveness, and sociability.
- **Skills.** Expertise required to do the job.

Easily remembered as C.A.P.S., this approach takes a
practical look at what's required. For each category, you
list and then rank in order of importance the factors that
make a jobholder exceptional, including situations and
examples of when each quality is called for.

In addition to producing a checklist, C.A.P.S. also
serves as a guide to what's important – from most to least
– when making a hiring decision.

The Best Employees

Capacities

If an applicant lacks the required capacities, nothing else matters.

The first thing to identify when creating a job checklist is capacity. There are two types of job-related capacities to consider:

- **Physical capacities.** Bending, lifting, reaching, climbing, hearing, seeing, etc. For each physical capacity required, indicate the nature and scope of the requirements in terms of distance, frequency, length of time spent doing it, weights, sizes, shape, etc. ("Ability to clearly see objects and people from a distance of 200 feet at night," might be a requirement for a convenience store employee.)

- **Mental capacities.** Define how much thinking and learning the job requires. Include specifics on the number of items or frequency of the duty and the knowledge and abilities required for success on the job. Mental capacities might include:
  1. Understand and carry out oral instructions.
  2. Understand and carry out written instructions.
  3. Read work orders, tickets, graphs, logs, schedules, etc.

4. Prepare detailed technical records or reports.
5. Inspect, examine, and observe for product, equipment, or workmanship defects.

The job analysis needs to be both site and shift specific. Conditions at different sites – size, physical barriers, layout, etc. – may require different capacities in order to perform the same job. Different shifts may require different capacities due to the time of day – opening or closing, for example, or total number of people working at the same time.

When hiring, capacities are the first and most important factors to consider. An applicant for a master technician's position had the best skills, attitudes, and personality, but was unable to do the job due to rheumatoid arthritis. The employer couldn't hire this applicant because he didn't have the required physical capacity.

If a job requires lifting and moving 60 pounds over a distance of 300 feet and the applicant can't physically do that, any other qualities the applicant may have make no difference. If a job requires talking on the phone and an applicant can't do that well, nothing else matters. Look for capacities first.

The Best Employees

Attitude

*The main reason employees fail isn't
because they can't do the job,
but because they won't.*

After capacity, the most important requirement is the right attitude. Research and countless employer surveys show that a good attitude is the most important quality an employee can have:

- A survey conducted by the Texas Workforce Commission asked 1,000 employers to identify the most important quality an employee can have. More than 85 percent named "positive attitude" or other specific attitudes such as honesty/integrity, ambition, dependability, and friendliness.

- When asked why they usually fire employees, only 9 percent of these employers said "inability to do the job." The rest cited attitude-related factors such as absenteeism and tardiness, bad attitude/work ethic, dishonesty/misconduct (69%) or "other reasons" (22%).

- According to the U.S. Department of Labor, more than 87 percent of employee failures are due to an unwillingness to do the job. Unwillingness is an attitude problem.

Where the needed capacities exist, positive attitude is what will determine success on the job. Without the right attitude, the person won't do well, no matter how proficient their skills. It's much easier to train an employee with a winning attitude to do the job than it is to try to train a grouch, who has the right experience and skills, to smile and be pleasant to your customers. This is why you should hire for attitude and train for skills.

Employee attitudes affect every company's success – especially in today's highly competitive business environment. Your employees are the ones who make the sales, make customers happy, and make them want to come back. Employees are also the ones who lose sales, upset customers, and make them stay away.

To your clients, your employees *are* the company and they need to have the right customer service attitudes. While you can train somebody in the skills needed to be a customer service representative, a candidate who doesn't believe the "customer is always right" won't ever do as well as someone who brings this attitude with them to the job every day.

By defining the attitudes that are most important for a jobholder's success, you can gear your hiring efforts toward those qualities.

The best way to get rid of a bad attitude is not to hire it in the first place.

The Best Employees

Personality

*There's no such thing
as a perfect match.*

It's wonderful if you can find the right personality when hiring, but, in reality, there will never be a perfect match.

For one thing, there are actually three personality fits involved. The new hire's personality and:

- the job's personality
- the manager's personality
- the company's personality

Few – if any – people will match all three, but the closer the match, the better the candidate.

The most important factor is how closely the applicant's personality matches the job – attention to detail, working with people, assertiveness, and competitiveness, for instance. People tend to do better at things that come naturally and that they enjoy doing.

When it comes to personality, the real issue is whether the person will manage his or her personality to get the job done or not. Every day, successful people do things on the job that they don't really like to do because they're able to manage their personalities. You'd probably rather be doing something other than reading this book right now, for example, but you're willing to spend some time, effort, and energy to increase your ability to hire effectively. Successful people manage their personalities and do the things that unsuccessful people don't like to do.

Notice the key is *managing* – not changing – personality to get the job done. Scientists tell us that about 60 percent of our personality is genetic and that most personality traits are embedded by age nine. In other words, personality is part of our basic wiring; it can't be taught and it doesn't change much over time.

The Best Employees

Skills

The ability to read is a skill;
the ability to learn to read is a capacity.

Employers who always put skills first when hiring are making a big mistake. While specific expertise may seem to be exactly what's needed, other factors even more profoundly affect business success. A person with the right capacities and attitudes can be trained in the needed skills. The desired capacities and attitudes, however, can't be taught. Remember, the preferred rule is to hire for attitude, train for skills.

Some jobs, however, do require certain skills and these can be as important as capacities and attitudes – especially if you're hiring a pilot for the corporate jet. Also, if there's no time or way to train and you need to hire now, your top two priorities become capacities and skills. The right attitude and personality fit would be a bonus, but it can sometimes be more important to hire someone who doesn't need training.

Skills are the easiest job requirements to identify and verify. If you need someone to drive a forklift, operate a cash register, or do data entry, you can easily list the expertise required to do the job and test for it. Testing for required skills should take place very early in the hiring process – and always before interviews – so you don't spend any unnecessary time with unqualified applicants.

Recruiting

Overview

The best you can hire is only the best of those who apply.

The second reason we don't have the best employees is that we don't know where to find them. The best people don't just walk up and ask you for a job. In most cases, they already have one – especially in a tight labor market. Even when the labor supply is plentiful, superior performers are difficult to come by. If you want the best, you have to know where and how to look for them.

Your guide in this search is the C.A.P.S. (Capacity, Attitude, Personality, Skills) analysis. With a detailed profile of the qualities and capabilities best suited for the job, you can target your recruiting toward people with those qualifications.

But traditional efforts usually won't work. People who already have jobs don't read help-wanted ads in the newspaper classifieds or notice "Now Hiring" signs. If you want quality people who will help your business prosper and grow, you must use every means possible to get them to apply.

Tap into new sources by directing your efforts to places where the people you want to attract are likely to be – where they congregate, socialize, go for entertainment, work, play, shop, live, get information, participate in the community, and search for common services.

Be creative in the ways you get their attention:

- An air conditioning repair company in Houston needed new technicians – in July! All potential candidates weren't only employed, but were too busy to do anything else but work, eat, and sleep. By advertising on a billboard across the street from the air conditioning supply house, however, the company heard from 22 qualified applicants in one week.

- A food-stamp distribution company needed people to work the first week of every month at minimum wage. Through careful analysis of its needs, the company decided to publicize the job openings to senior mall walkers. The result was a higher quantity and quality of people than the company ever imagined being able to hire for the job.

- When trying to recruit new employees, a business that hires and caters to teenagers thought about where teens spend time on weekends. Movie theaters seemed to be the answer, so the company bought advertising space on the screens at local theaters. It worked, attracting some great job applicants – and many new customers as well.

- A company that hires college students recruits through local college radio stations, campus newspapers, the college placement office, billboards on campus, fraternities, and sororities.

- You can even create a place for applicants to congregate and socialize:

  1. A grocery store that conducts a fastest-sacker contest, for example, uses it as much as a recruiting tool as a public relations activity.

  2. A restaurant in Orlando – a city known for recruiting problems because of the famous employer there – invites all local hospitality industry employees for $1 beer and free chicken wings every Sunday night from 10:30 p.m. to 1 a.m. The restaurant manager gets 300-500 experienced, potential applicants to visit his establishment once a week. He doesn't have a recruiting problem and hasn't had to run an ad in more than three years.

Recruiting

Targeting

*The times demand new thinking and
new approaches to recruiting.*

When you think in terms of actively and creatively targeting your recruiting efforts, the possibilities are practically endless. Here are more than 90 ways to recruit – without using the classifieds:

Schools
Trade
Vocational
Real estate
Continuing and adult
    education
Universities
Junior and community
    colleges
Skills centers
College dorms
Technical schools
Aviation schools
High-school intern
    programs

Media
Cable TV
Billboards
Internet/your website
News releases
Display ads in newspaper
Bus benches
Bus signs
Bus-shelter signs
Yellow pages
Tear-off bulletin board signs
Direct mail
Doorknob signs
Chamber of Commerce
    directories
Payroll stuffers
Invoice stuffers
Radio ads
Talk radio shows

Media *(cont.)*
Job service directory
Balloons
Airplane banners
Church bulletins
Movie-theater screens

Referrals
Current employees
Job services
Churches/synagogues
Customers
Military recruiting offices
YM/YWCA
Social clubs
Military base housing
Senior centers
Retirement communities
Vocational/rehab
    counselors
Goodwill
Fellowship house
Service Core of Retired
    Executives
Foreign consulates
Relocation specialists
Teachers
Student services on
    campuses
Out-placement agencies
Talent agencies
Personnel agencies
Former employees

Community Groups
Bowling leagues
Parents without Partners
Displaced homemakers
Church groups
Sororities
Fraternities
Youth groups
Condominium associations
4H clubs
Consulate lists
Ethnic newspapers
Neighborhood recruiters
Purchased lists
Fliers at high-traffic areas
Sandwich-board walker
Garden clubs
Companies downsizing
Coupon mailing programs
Community grocery stores
"How to get a job" seminars
Contests and Job fairs
Booth at craft shows
Public Service Announcements
Job hotlines
Public speaking
Newsletters
Signs in daycare centers
AARP ads
Car window fliers
Mobile recruiting vehicle
Shopping center kiosk
Open house
Remote recruiting
Ad in personals column
Welcome Wagon
Sponsor a community event

Recruiting

Take a Marketing Approach

*You should always be looking
for your next employee.*

If you only recruit when you have a job opening, you can't get the best. Waiting to recruit until you need someone is like grocery shopping on an empty stomach – you'll buy the first thing that looks good and doesn't need to be cooked. Feeling pressured to hire someone causes you to be less selective and often results in a bad hiring decision.

Recruiting should be an on-going process. You should recruit new employees the same way you market to attract new customers – proactively and consistently. This is why employment agencies always have people; they're always recruiting. What gets measured, gets done, so set a goal for the number of applications you'll collect or interviews you'll conduct every week or month – especially when you don't have openings to fill. By taking a proactive, marketing approach to recruiting, you'll build a database of potential applicants.

While more applicants is better, you still need more than simply an increased number of choices. You need to attract more applicants who meet your criteria. With a greater quantity and higher quality of applicants in your database, you'll increase your chances of finding the best employees when you need them.

Recruiting

Marketing Communications

All recruiting is advertising;
all advertising is recruiting.

Recruiting and advertising are one in the same. One good example of doing this right is, "Come see the softer side of Sears™." Whether you're selling products and services to your customers or employment opportunities to potential applicants, you're sending out messages about your organization:

- Every time you advertise, you're not only attracting potential customers, you're also sending out recruiting messages that will either make people want to work for you or not. A bar that sponsors a sports show on cable TV, for example, is advertising as much that it's a good place to work as it's advertising that it's a good place to socialize.

- Whenever you recruit, your recruiting message influences people to want – or not want – to do business with your company. Consider the ubiquitous "Now Hiring" sign. The message it conveys to customers is that the business doesn't have enough employees to provide good service. If you hang it out often enough, it says you can't keep good people. A message like "Come Grow with Us," however, suggests success and growth and attracts customers and job applicants alike.

- Be conscious of the message given by everything an applicant sees, including ads, application forms, and company facilities. Your
  company should always put its best foot forward. (At a job fair, one company stocked its
  booth with low-quality photocopies of its application form. Such an uncaring and sloppy
  image attracts uncaring and sloppy employees.)
- Understand that, in the eye of the beholder,
  recruiting is about image. You need to know
  applicants' perceptions of your industry,
  your competition, your company, and specific jobs, so you can deal with them accordingly.

Recruiting

Make It Easy

If you want to hire the best, make it easy for people to apply.

If you accept phone calls, résumés, and applications only during normal work hours, you're discouraging the very people you should be trying to recruit. Most people who are working can only comfortably respond after hours.

- Modify or extend your hours for accepting applications and for conducting interviews to coincide with applicant availability. If two restaurants next to each other display "Help-Wanted" signs, one advertising that interviews are conducted between 3 and 5 p.m. and the other conducting interviews anytime, which will get more applicants?

- Install a 24-hour job hotline[1] and publicize it everywhere you recruit. It can be as simple as an answering machine or as sophisticated as a fully automated interviewing system. By doing this, you'll get at least 30-50 percent more high-quality applicants. (In three weeks of advertising for convenience store clerks, one company received only two responses. In just the first week of including a "24-hour job hotline" phone number in its ad, the company received 26 qualified responses.)

---

[1] To sample a computerized job hotline, call 1-800-348-0008.

Recruiting

The Magnetic Company®

If they don't want to work for you,
nobody's gonna stop 'em.[2]

There are companies that never have recruiting problems. When they need good employees, plenty of candidates are readily available. Disney, Nordstrom, Southwest Airlines, Compaq, Saturn, and Proctor & Gamble are some examples. People hear all the time that these are good places to work, so people want to work for them. Many small, local companies across the country have similar reputations. In fact, being small can be an advantage. These companies can use the flexibility inherent to their smaller size to become a Magnetic Company®.

How do you become a Magnetic Company®? By giving employees what they want – not in terms of the highest pay, best benefits, or being easy to work for, but in terms of appreciation, challenge, growth, and opportunity. It's about recognizing that people are important to the organization and treating them accordingly. *Magnetic companies naturally attract, select, and retain the best – and repel the rest* – because they:

- Treat employees with respect.
- Have rules and apply those rules fairly.
- Communicate to employees what employees need and want to know.
- Listen to employees.
- Are flexible.

---

[2] With a tip of the hat to Yogi Berra.

- Give employees the tools they need to do the job well.
- Reward excellence.
- Make work fun.
- Manage people the way they want to be managed (not the way the managers might prefer).
- Recognize employees' abilities and potential and have a plan for maximizing the best of what they have.
- Don't accept mediocrity.

Just as you don't always have to have the lowest price for customers to prefer your products or services, you don't have to pay the most to be a Magnetic Company®.

Being a Magnetic Company® doesn't mean you're easy to work for either. It means having high standards and high expectations that are rewarded when met. It means doing a lot of little things better.

People do things for their own reasons, not yours. What gets you out of bed for work in the morning is not necessarily what motivates your best employees. Help them get what they want and they'll help you get what you want – more of the kinds of employees who attract and retain the customers who will grow your business. If you apply all the rules you normally use for customer care to employee care, you'll have what it takes to become a Magnetic Company®.

Recruiting

Former Employees

*Is the grass really greener
on the other side?*

When employees quit to go work somewhere else, they often discover that the grass isn't greener after all. In fact, research shows that 20 to 25 percent of supervisory and managerial employees have gone back to work at a company they once left.

Imagine if 20 percent of all the good people who ever left came back to work for you! You'd have instantaneously productive workers, requiring little or no job training, and little or no downtime to become familiar with the organization.

- All you have to do is ask. One or two months after someone good leaves, just call and ask if he or she would consider coming back. The worst they could say is "no," and you've just given them a wonderful compliment. What's so bad about that?

- Or, like the Domino's manager who went to the homes of eight former employees, you could personally visit them. (Five came back to work for him.)

- Even if the answer is "no," former employees can be valuable sources for referrals. Simply ask, "Do you know anybody else who might fit our organization who you would recommend to us?"
- Of course, to do this, you have to be able to get in touch with former employees. One way is to keep them on mailing lists for employee newsletters and other corporate communications.

Recruiting

Capitalize on Current Employees

The second-best source of recruits
is all the good people who
work for you now.

Research shows that employee-referred candidates are three times more likely to be a good match for the job. This is because your employees give these candidates much more detailed information about the job requirements and working conditions than you would. As a result, candidates are only likely to proceed with the selection process if they feel they will fit the job. And because they're a good fit, referral candidates who are hired are also much less likely to quit or be fired within the first few months.

The key is to let employees know that you need good people and what you're looking for. If you don't already have one, consider implementing a referral incentive or bonus program for employees and:

- Make sure all employees know about it and understand how to participate.

- Make it fun and create some excitement. Programs that award bonuses of $100 or $250, but don't pay anything until the new employee has been on the job for six months don't get employees excited about participating. But a program that awards all, or at least half, the bonus amount on the new employee's first day – in cash – and makes it an event, gets maximum bang for the buck. An exciting award presentation will generate a lot of attention and interest from those who attend. The employee who made the referral gets recognition for helping the organization grow and prosper. And high expectations are established for the new employee to do well because he or she was referred by an established employee.

- Other ways to add excitement to a referral program include giving employees a choice between cash and a day off with pay; making it a game (a drawing from a variety of prizes, a "wheel of fortune," or a departmental contest). Whatever will excite your people and get them involved.

Recruiting

Applicants as Sources

*The third-best source is every applicant
who walks through the door.*

Professional recruiters report they get some of their best applicants from the people they interview. You can too.

Ask every applicant you interview for the names and phone numbers of several people they've worked with, as well as people they've worked for. Then call those they've worked with and mention that the applicant listed them as "personal references." This serves two purposes:

- You can get as much information about the reference's qualities and abilities as you do about the applicant. If you like what you hear, add their name to your potential-applicant database. When you need someone like that in the future, you can call them back, remind them of your previous conversation and mention there are new openings you thought they might be interested in.

- Since no one told these people not to tell you anything, you'll probably get more honest, substantial information about the applicant's capacities, attitudes, personality traits, and skills (C.A.P.S.) than you will from supervisory references.

Recruiting

Advertising

*"Help Wanted" is not a reason
for anybody to apply.*

Advertising is the fourth-best recruiting method – if it's done right. The right way starts with writing an ad that attracts the quantity and quality of applicants you need. Your ad needs to answer, up front, the reasons why the people you're trying to attract would want to work for you.

The headline must grab the attention of the people you're trying to attract and get them to read further. "Help Wanted" just doesn't cut it, but here are some headlines that will:

"Success starts with . . ."
"Come grow with us."
"Nobody else gives you the opportunities we do."
"Tired of . . .?"
"Turn your career around."
"Use your talent."
"Invest in yourself."
"You deserve the best – and so do we."
"Take the first step toward a better future."
"Starting out or starting over?"
"Get in on the ground floor."
"No more rush hour blues."
"The opportunity you've been waiting for . . ."
"A few good reasons to talk to us . . ."

The rest of the ad must present the job and its requirements as clearly and precisely as possible, screening in those who are qualified and screening out those who aren't. Basic elements include:

- **Who.** The name of the company and description of the ideal candidate.

- **What.** Job title and brief (one sentence) description of job duties and responsibilities.

- **When.** Times during which applicants should respond in person, by phone, fax, or e-mail, and the deadline for responding.

- **Where.** Address or general location of the job.

- **Why.** The reason the job is open if it's due to expansion, growth, or internal promotion.

- **How.** Exact procedures for applying.

- **How much.** While salary is always important to the reader, only include it if you're sure that your salary range is competitive.

- **Drug policy.** To make sure drug users don't apply, include a statement about your company's intolerance of drug use, such as "Must be drug free," or "We are a drug free workforce."

Remember, the goal of ad writing is to attract "a buyer." Sell the company and job by using relevant and compelling words in the body of the ad. When describing job duties and responsibilities, use active verbs, such as "create," "explore," "launch," "specialize." When describing the candidate, company, and job, use interesting nouns and adjectives, such as "dynamic," "ingenious," "prestigious," "versatile," "winning."

Make sure the message and words appeal to your target market. Include positive features and benefits from the candidate's point of view; highlight aspects of the job that would attract superior performers. A moving company that wanted to attract people who work out had great success with "Earn While You Burn."

Continuously assess the effectiveness of your ads in attracting the type of people you want. When interviewing candidates, ask what made them respond to the ad, then use their feedback to improve future ads.

Change your headlines (and store signage) frequently to ensure you have a diverse pool of applicants to select from. If you always run the same message, you'll always get the same types of people.

Recruiting

Advertising

Three-line ads attract three-line applicants.

No matter how well written an ad is, it won't be effective if it isn't seen by the people you're trying to attract.

To get response from top performers not actively looking for a new job, your ad has to jump out at them. Small, poorly designed ads are easily overlooked, especially when "help-wanted" is the biggest section of the newspaper. If you scrimp on size and design, you'll cheat yourself out of the high-quality candidates you seek and end up spending a lot of time and money on unqualified applicants.

Your ad also needs to be seen frequently enough to attract good response. It doesn't always have to be the same size, but the more often there's something for people to see, the better. This frequency applies not only from week to week in the newspaper, but also within one edition. For example, the same ad could be run in several different job-category listings or smaller ads in other categories could refer readers to the large display ad.

Actual placement can also make or break the response an ad generates. Since people who already have jobs don't normally read the classifieds, try advertising in different sections of the newspaper. Think in terms of what your target audience is likely to read:

- Advertise job openings for real estate offices in the real-estate section; travel agencies in the travel section; auto mechanics in the automotive section.

Even when the help-wanted section is the appropriate – or only – choice, the specific category can make a difference. Consider the company that needed apprentice carpenters. The jobs started at $5.50 per hour, increasing to $18 an hour at the end of the three-year training program. The original ad drew only three or four responses when placed in the "craft labor" category of the classifieds. When the ad ran in the "restaurant" section with the attention-getting headline, "Are you tired of dirty dishes?" it attracted 300 responses.

The best day of the week to advertise a job opening is Sunday. Avoid Friday, Saturday, Monday, and three- or four-day (holiday) weekends.

Recruiting

Recruiting Cards

*Don't leave home
without 'em.*

An easy way to make recruiting an ongoing activity is to create and use a recruiting card. It looks like a business card, but has a recruiting message on it like: "Great service! We're always looking for good employees like you." The card invites the recipient to call for a confidential interview and includes pertinent contact information.

This can be printed on the back of your regular card or you can create a specialized card where the second side tells potential recruits why they should call:

The Hire Tough Group Offers Great Perks Including:

Casual Fridays

Free Sodas, Candy, & Popcorn Every Day

Free Bagels on Fridays (with cream cheese)

A Party & Presents on Your Birthday!

ALL THIS PLUS:

Regular Paychecks and L–O–N–G Hours!

Always carry the cards with you and give them to people who provide you with exceptional service or demonstrate outstanding qualities and abilities.

- If you can, as an added incentive, include a discount or giveaway offer on a product or service. When someone redeems a card, get the person's name and phone number so you can add it to your database of potential applicants.

- At a restaurant, always ask to be seated at the best employee's station. You'll not only enjoy your meal more, but you may find your next employee. Since the employee doesn't know he or she is being evaluated, you'll get an accurate picture of his or her performance.

- At a fast-food restaurant, order a beverage, take a seat, and watch for the best employees.

Recruiting

Your Community

*For some of the best candidates,
look in your own backyard.*

Great sources of applicants are as close and convenient as local community and networking groups. Don't overlook or underestimate these possibilities in your community:

- Chambers of Commerce
- Trade and professional organizations
- Churches and synagogues
- School functions
- Daycare centers (the children's parents)
- Social clubs
- Bowling leagues
- Support groups
- Art and cultural events
- Newcomers' groups

Recruiting

Personnel Agencies & Recruiters

Personnel professionals:
make them work for you!

As long as you're aware of their limitations, personnel agencies and recruiters can be helpful in finding applicants. Not all, however, are as concerned as you are about making the best possible match between job and candidate. Some agencies tend to care more about sales than results.

- The turnover rate in the personnel agency industry is about 90 percent, so the representative servicing your account may be new to the agency or new to the business.
- The lower the rate you negotiate, the less attention your account is likely to receive.
- Your contact recruiter isn't necessarily the person who will actually do the recruiting; make sure you know who the players are.

Also, consider the following alternatives that have become increasingly popular:

- **Temp-to-permanent.** You pay an agency to hire a person on its payroll as a temporary worker for a certain period of time. At the end of that period, if you're sure the person is what you need, you hire him or her as a permanent employee on your payroll. If the employee isn't what you need, you have no further obligation.

- **Employee leasing.** Employees technically work for the agency, but are leased to you. This arrangement offers convenience because the agency handles payroll, benefits, and other administrative matters. The drawback, however, is if employee leasing isn't used throughout your organization, it may send a message to employees who are "leased" that they are somehow less important.

Recruiting

Non-Traditional

It's time to do some out-of-the-box thinking.

Due to economic expansion and population shifts, there are more jobs to be filled than there are young people with the necessary skills to fill them. Here are some non-traditional groups employers should consider as traditional sources dry up:

- **Older people.** Their wealth of work and life experience usually far exceeds whatever the job requires, so you get much more for your money. To recruit them, go to where they are – senior's housing developments, volunteer organizations, mall walking – even Bingo games.

- **Physically and mentally challenged people.** It's not only the right thing – morally and legally – to do, but it's smart. Track records prove that physically and mentally challenged people are good workers, requiring only minimal accommodations. One source is the National Telecommuting Institute (NTI). It offers nationwide training and supervision to individuals with disabilities who want to work from home. NTI can get workers the computer equipment and phones they need and companies participating in the program are entitled to a federal tax credit for hiring individuals with disabilities. For more information, go to www.caes.mit.edu/vc/nti.

- **Welfare recipients.** There's a lot of talk about welfare-to-work programs aimed at getting the so-called "unemployable" employed. It involves more than placing people in jobs however. Usually basic training in good work ethics is required. Most small companies can't afford to do what it takes to hire, train, and assimilate people who have never worked. However, there is some incentive. The Small Business Job Protection Act of 1996 authorized the Work Opportunity Tax Credit (WOTC) Program to help move people from welfare to work. By hiring certain job seekers, employers can reduce their federal tax liability by as much as $2,100 per qualified new worker or $1,050 per qualified summer youth. If you're interested, you can sign up on-line at www.sba.gov/welfare, the Small Business Administration's web site.

- **Parolees.** Several states will provide bond for hired ex-cons and some, such as Texas, even have work-release programs which train and support parolees entering the workforce. A major drawback, however, is that employers have to be especially careful about negligent hiring lawsuits.

- **Full-time employees looking for a second job.** More than seven million people in the United States hold at least two jobs at once. To attract them, recruiting efforts should emphasize a second income, flexible hours, and other benefits that would appeal to people working more than one job.

- **Parents with young children.** Full-time workers may be interested in part-time work in order to be home more often with their children. A great place to recruit them is through daycare centers near your location where they drop off and pick up their children.

- **Newcomers.** People moving into your neighborhood may be very interested in working close to home. Even those who moved in because of a job they already have might have a spouse who's looking for work. Realtors and your local Welcome Wagon are great sources for these recruits.

Recruiting

Self-Audit

*Take an honest look at your
recruiting practices.*

Determine where you are and how you can improve
so you have an ongoing supply of qualified applicants:

- **Good Recruiting.** You actively market your
  company to the workforce on a regular
  schedule, regardless of current hiring needs.

- **Better Recruiting.** You increase your applicant quality and quantity, while decreasing
  your investments in terms of time, money,
  lost productivity, etc.

- **Best Recruiting.** You set a recruiting goal
  and apply as many recruiting methods and
  systems as possible. This results in a broader
  and more diverse applicant base, as well as
  more candidates of a higher quality.

A good self-audit would review these areas for possible improvement:

- Do we see applicants arrive from a good mix
  of sources?

- How many applicants are we getting for each
  job opening?

- How large is our applicant pool (applicants
  ready to call, if needed)?

- How much money are we currently spending
  on recruiting?

- How much are we paying recruiters?
- Do our managers have recruiting goals?
- Is there enough cultural diversity in the applicant pool?
- How many hours do we actively recruit per week?
- What recruiting information are we obtaining from applicants?
- What recruiting information are we obtaining from present employees?
- On average, how long does it take to replace an employee?
- On average, what does it cost to replace an employee?

Recruiting

Why Bother?

*If you continue doing what you're doing,
you'll continue to get what you got.*

Here are just a few of the problems resulting from in-effective recruiting:

- Increases both short- and long-term management stress.
- Increases cost-per-hire and downtime losses.
- You end up hiring a warm body instead of the best person for the job.
- Leaves the decision up to chance or luck.
- Increases turnover, since you're not finding the right people to begin with.
- Decreases productivity and internal morale.
- Increases overtime.
- You'll need to do it over and over and over again.

When you invest some time up front to create a system that works for you, the benefits of an on-going recruiting program include:

- Shortens downtime when jobs need to be filled.
- Saves time and money.
- Makes managing easier.
- Reduces cost per hire.
- Reduces turnover.

- Increases the cultural diversity necessary for success.
- Increases revenues and profits because you have the right people.
- Increases chances of successful hiring.
- Adds value to your organization now and in the future because you're recruiting the people who will be your competitive advantage.

In other words, it makes you and your organization more productive and successful.

Selection Systems

Overview

*The three keys to great hiring are
systems, systems, systems.*

The third reason we don't have the best employees is because we don't know how to determine who really is the best. Once we have applicants, we need a way to figure out which ones are really right for the job and the organization.

In most cases, employers form impressions and make all their decisions during the interview. University of Chicago research tells us that decisions based on interviews alone are only five percent better than those made by flipping a coin. "Heads, I hire you; tails, I don't." Is this any way to run a business?

To increase the odds in your favor you have to gather information in more than one way, from more than one source, and at more than one time. It takes a multi-step system that uses more of the applicant's time and less of yours to determine who is truly the best.

After all, don't you have systems for just about everything else? Compensation, ordering, payroll, inventory, accounting, and quality control systems provide the structures that make things happen effectively and efficiently – every time. You need a system for selecting the people who will best contribute to your success.

Many variables determine exactly what a hiring system looks like. Every organization has its own needs and often the type of position determines how the system works. Outside factors, such as the economic environment and availability of applicants may also influence the specific tools and procedures used. While there's no one-size-fits-all hiring system, the basic components of an effective system are:

- **Describe the Job.** Develop a job analysis – define the capacities, attitudes, personality traits, and skill (C.A.P.S.) requirements – so you know what you need.

- **Recruit.** Look for applicants in an on-going, proactive manner.

- **Gather Information.** Through a combination of methods and sources, collect as much pertinent information as possible about applicants. There are two ways to get information – actively and passively (in person and on paper) – and two sources of information (the applicant and anyone else who can tell you something about the applicant).

- **Evaluate.** Use all the information you've gathered to evaluate and compare candidates.

Selection Systems

Hire Tough

Hire tough. Manage easy.

Essentially, there are only two ways to handle the hiring process and far too many organizations take the "hire easy" approach – especially when it comes to hourly employees.

Hire easy means applicants need merely pass a pulse test in order to start work. "Got a heartbeat? You're hired."

When an employer puts such little value on the job, that's exactly the value and effort employees will put into the job. They'll be poor performers and problem employees who require constant attention. Their employers will need to have exceptional management skills – and stamina. The less you expect in the hiring process and the easier the job is to get, the more time and money you're going to spend trying to get the people you hire to do what you need them to do.

The reverse is also true. The harder the job is to get, the better the quality of the people you attract and the easier and less time-consuming the manager's job becomes. When you hire tough, more of the best people will want to be on your team.

This is because people who take pride in their work and abilities will also work hard to get a job. People who don't will deselect themselves by dropping out or performing poorly.

Hiring tough is also one of the prime characteristics of a Magnetic Company®. People figure a company that takes the hiring process seriously must be a good place to work. People stand in long lines to get jobs at Disney World for minimum wage – to work outside in the hot summer sun! Even though they know the jobs are hard to get, people do it because they've heard that you have to be the best to work there.

So the challenge is to build a system that makes the job hard to get and helps you hire more effectively – and quickly, especially in a tight labor market. Hiring tough doesn't mean a long process. It means having a system that enables you to make decisions in one day, so you don't lose good applicants when there are plenty of job opportunities.

Selection Systems

This is a Test

Everything you do in the
hiring process is a test.

Hiring tough doesn't mean being overbearing, rude, or insensitive to applicants. It simply means having a system that gathers as much useful information as possible about them – using their time, not yours.

The beauty of such a system is underscored by the fact that, according to the U.S. government, everything we do in the hiring process is a test:

- If you need a customer service representative who will have a lot of phone contact with your customers, one of the first steps in your hiring process should be a phone conversation with the applicant. If the person's phone manner and attitude don't impress you, he or she certainly won't impress your customers.

- Requesting a cover letter or specific information in your help wanted ad is another test. If the information is not provided, the applicant flunks the test.

- If writing skills are required for the job, test for them by including essay questions on the application.

- If the job requires starting work at 5:00 a.m., schedule the interview at that time to test the applicant's ability and willingness to be on time for work.

- If you need someone with a friendly attitude and that type of attitude isn't displayed during the interview, the applicant fails that test.

- Paper-and-pencil or computerized tests can measure all sorts of things – capacities, attitudes, personality, and skills (C.A.P.S.).

By looking at every step of the process like it's a test, you'll stay focused on what's most important to the position and you'll get the most pertinent information. The more tests applicants pass, the more compatible and successful they'll be in the job and the easier they'll be to manage. Testing screens in the best.

Selection System Tools

Overview

*The more you know,
the less you risk.*

When it comes to the information-gathering component of a hiring system, more is better.

The more information you have on applicants, the better the chances you'll make a good hiring decision and avoid all the costs and hassle of having to do it over again – and again, and again.

There are two ways to gather information – direct contact with applicants, such as interviewing, and through the use of tools like:

- **Employment application.** Records pertinent information in an organized, standardized format.

- **Résumé.** Presents information the applicant wants you to know.

- **Pre-screening questions.** Help determine whether an applicant meets the basic qualifications of the job or not.

- **Testing.** Since everything in the hiring process can be viewed as a test, you have both formal and informal testing opportunities.

- **Demonstration release.** Releases you from liability when the applicant meets your request to show that he or she can physically do the job.

- **Structured interview.** Establishes a sequence of questions that's specific to the job you're trying to fill.
- **Reference verification.** Gives you permission to get information about the applicant.
- **Reference release.** Gives you permission to provide information about the applicant if you should employ him or her.

In most organizations, the only tools used are applications and résumés, but, in reality, the possibilities are endless. Once you know what you're looking for, you can find or design the tools to help you get it. And like all good tools, when used properly, hiring tools get the job done with a minimum of time and effort.

Selection System Tools

Employment Applications

The most important piece of paper between you and an applicant is the employment application.

The employment application[3] is the best way to collect the information you want and need to know about each applicant. While it's often a balancing act between getting what you want and being legally and politically correct about it, developing a good application form is worth the effort.

- **It is an important test in the hiring process.** By instructing applicants to fill it out completely – leaving no blanks and not writing "see résumé" anywhere – you're testing whether or not they follow instructions and read, write, and understand English. If someone fails this test because of an unwillingness or inability to follow instructions, why spend any more time with this applicant?

- **It's a legal document.** You're required to have a completed application form for each applicant and to keep it on file for at least one year. (In some cases, it's up to three years, so be sure to check your state law.)

- **Don't write anything on it.** Since these are legal documents that have to be kept on file, any notations on them about the applicant

---

[3] See sample Employment Application on page 154 of the Tool Kit.

could later be held against you in court. Delete any "Comments" section on your application form and never write your impressions or thoughts on them.

- **Make sure it doesn't include any illegal, discriminatory items.** For example, asking for the date the person graduated from high school leaves you vulnerable to age discrimination suits. Asking for marital status may suggest a preference; stating that employees become "permanent" after a 90-day probation raises contract issues. It's easier to leave such items out rather than defend yourself in court.

- **Make sure applicants complete them on site.** Don't mail applications or allow people to take them home. If you do, you have no way of knowing if the applicant was actually the person who filled it out.

- **Give an application out to everyone who asks.** If you give out applications only to some people, you're leaving yourself open to discrimination charges.

- **Require every applicant to complete your application.** No matter what job they're applying for, even if they've already submitted a résumé, get a completed application. This ensures you have orderly and consistent information on everyone and makes it easy to quickly find the information you need and make logical comparisons.

Selection System Tools

Evaluating Applications

*A completed employment application reveals
a lot about the applicant.*

When reviewing an application, there are five areas to consider:

- **Clarity**
    1. How clear are the answers and explanations to questions?
    2. Were the instructions followed?
    3. Did the applicant hurry through the form or take the time to do it right?
    4. Were the questions answered with applicable, up-to-date information?

- **Cleanliness** (These factors are indicative of how organized and attentive to detail the applicant may be on the job.)
    1. Did the applicant take special care to keep the application clean and neat?
    2. Was it folded up, wrinkled, or ripped?
    3. Does it have stains or smudges on it?

- **Legibility**
    1. Is the handwriting neat and easy to read?
    2. Does it fit in the lines?
    3. Can you understand what the applicant is trying to communicate?

    4. Are there many cross-outs or era-
       sures?

- **Experience**

    1. Does the experience presented match
       the experience required for the job?
    2. Do you get a good idea of a person's
       previous duties and responsibilities
       from the descriptions?

- **Education**

    1. Is it consistent with the years and
       types of employment?
    2. Are the courses relevant to the posi-
       tion?
    3. Has the person completed the re-
       quired level of education?
    4. Is it credible?

Selection System Tools

Application Waivers & Releases[4]

The employment application form is most important for the rights it protects – yours.

Making sure everyone completes an employment application ensures you have a signed waiver from all applicants. This waiver should include these statements that protect the employer's right to:

- Regard false, misleading, or omitted information on the application (and any supporting documentation) as immediate grounds for reprimand or dismissal.

- Establish an employment-at-will policy, meaning employees can be fired for any or no reason – as long as it's not discriminatory and doesn't violate any other statutes. (Check what applies in your states of operation – it varies.)

- Distinguish the application from being an offer of employment. Unless you specifically state that the application isn't an employment offer, giving it to applicants could be interpreted that way.

- Perform a reference check and free anyone from being held liable for releasing such information to you.

---

[4]See sample Employment Application waivers and releases in the Tool Kit section on pages 154-155.

- Give references on terminated employees. The waiver holds you harmless for giving out truthful information.

- Require a physical examination after a conditional job offer is made.

- Conduct drug tests any time prior to or during employment.

- Release medical information on employees involved in job-related accidents and other situations.

- Change wages and benefits at any time.

- Refer employment-related disputes to binding arbitration. (This may be a quicker, more effective, less expensive, and less painful alternative to litigation).

Conducting a background check by securing the right to check criminal, credit, and other records may require separate forms. (Consult legal counsel conversant with applicable state and federal requirements.)

Selection System Tools

Résumés

*The only thing you learn from a résumé
is how good the applicant's
creative writing skills are.*

There are so many résumé-writing programs and services these days that you have no way of knowing how much effort and truth an individual actually put into those that come across your desk. Even if it's the person's own work, it is still suspect. After all, the reason people prepare résumés is to gain entrance to the hiring process. Résumés are packed with the information the writer wants you to know with a spin on whatever makes the applicant look best.

Sometimes the spin is very creative. Consider the résumé that listed the following as an accomplishment on a previous job: "reorganized the entire office." When asked about it, the interviewer found the candidate had simply moved a file cabinet from one wall to another. Or, how about the salesman who claimed his performance put him "at the top in sales" at his company? Come to find out, there was a grand total of three salespeople on staff.

Studies show that up to 70 percent of résumés contain false, inaccurate, or misleading information. This doesn't mean you should totally disregard or discount résumés as a hiring tool, but it does mean you should be careful about how you use them:

- **Require a cover letter.** Always specify that a cover letter, with certain information, be submitted with a résumé. It forces the applicant to write the letter and it will probably reveal more about the applicant than you'll ever get from the résumé.

- **Read it from back to front.** You'll be less likely to overlook the applicant's weak points, which are usually at the end.

- **Look for employment gaps.** While they may be legitimate (due to an economic downturn, a spouse's relocation, etc.), there could be other reasons, such as incarceration or employment failure.

- **Use it along with the application blank.** Remember, everyone should be required to complete an application to ensure you have consistent, orderly information on all applicants. The application also serves as a check and balance against the résumé.

Selection System Tools

Telephone Screening

*The shortest distance between you
and an applicant is the phone.*

Once you have an application that looks good, whenever possible, your first real contact with the applicant should be by phone. It can be as short as just asking a few key questions or as long as a complete, in-depth interview. (A longer phone conversation may be appropriate if extensive communication skills are important to the job or if geographic restrictions warrant, but the phone is still a screening tool and should never replace an in-person interview.)

The benefits of telephone screening include:

- If the applicant doesn't meet the job's minimum qualifications, you can quickly eliminate the person without investing any more time.

- It makes it easy for the person to apply.

- If the job requires the use of the phone, it becomes a primary test.

- It reduces your legal exposure. If you don't see the applicant, it's unlikely you'll be accused of discrimination.

Selection System Tools

Automated Phone Screening[5]
Let the computer do the talking.

When conducted by an automated system, telephone screening can be even more effective and productive. Such a system communicates job opportunity information and obtains basic applicant screening information 24-hours a day, seven days a week – without human involvement. This allows you to more quickly screen out those who don't meet your basic criteria and respond to those who do. Because it can handle an unlimited number of job applicants, an automated system maximizes your recruitment advertising return-on-investment.

Using an automated system also dramatically increases your chances of success. Since it's available at all times, people can easily apply at their convenience, thereby eliminating any stumbling blocks for all the good people who are already working.

---

[5] To sample an automated telephone screening system, call 1-800-348-0008.

Selection System Tools

Pre-Screening Questions

*Eliminate the turkeys so you
can focus on the eagles.*

To help you screen in qualified candidates and screen out the unqualified, develop a list of preliminary, pre-screening questions to ask applicants at the earliest possible stage in your hiring system. It's best to do this pre-screening by phone, but it can also be done in person.

Developing these questions from the job's C.A.P.S. (Capacities, Attitudes, Personality traits, and Skills) analysis will ensure you cover only essential capabilities and qualities. Depending on the job requirements, pre-screening questions might include:

- When are you available to start?
- Do you have reliable transportation?
- Do you have a valid driver's license?
- What days/shifts do you prefer to work?
- What days/shifts are you available to work? Which days/shifts would you prefer not to work?
- What is your minimum salary requirement?
- Can you lift 50 to 60 pounds on a repetitive basis?
- Have you ever been fired or asked to leave a job?
- If hired, how long do you plan to stay in this job?

Even if some of these questions are on the application, you may want to ask them by phone too as a check and balance. Just make sure you ask these questions *before* you tell applicants any specifics of the job. Otherwise, you're likely to hear what you've just told them you want to hear instead of accurate and honest information about the applicant's qualifications.

If applicants meet these basic requirements, ask them to come in for the next step in your selection system.

Selection System Tools

Testing

To get the best,
you have to test.

Paper and pencil or computerized testing software is a vastly under-used and under-valued tool:

- Compared to other information (academic achievement, experience, interviews, and references, etc.), test results more accurately predict success once on the job. In fact, "The interview, when used alone, is, on average, only about 8 percent more effective than flipping a coin." [6]

- Tests provide systemized, organized, validated information that facilitates better hiring decisions.

- Testing produces immediate results and insight into a candidate.

- Testing measures and verifies information provided on the application blank, résumé, and other pre-screening tools.

- Testing can uncover hidden qualities that weren't revealed through other tools.

---

[6] *Testing as a Predictor of Training Success and Job Performance,* Dr. John E. Hunter, Industrial Psychologist, Michigan State University, 1969.

- Testing can be a way to ask questions about drug use, theft, and other values that we are often uncomfortable asking in person.
- You can create or purchase a test to measure just about anything.
- Best of all, testing makes your system fair. Unsuccessful applicants don't feel your decision was based on race, age, marital status or any other bias.

Selection System Tools

When to Test

Test first, not last.

Whether it's for capacities, attitudes, personality, or skills, all testing is simply another way to interview the applicant. And the beauty is that it uses the applicant's time, not yours.

It's also the easiest way to get more of the information you need in order to make the best decision. (Remember, the more you know, the less you risk.)

Testing can give you validated information about intelligence, strength, stamina, dependability, honesty, drive, initiative, typing speed, and computer software proficiency – whatever it takes to get the job done. Testing gives you responses to hundreds of questions you'd never have time to ask – including the questions most of us don't like to ask in person, especially when it comes to attitudes and personality.

Testing should be done as early in the selection process as makes sense for your organization. Some make the mistake of testing last – thinking, perhaps, they're saving money this way. This is a no-win situation. Every applicant who has passed the preliminary tests you use (résumé with cover letter, application, phone screen, prescreening questions) should be tested before interviews.

If you don't test until after you've conducted an interview that you feel went well:

- You waste your time. You don't know who "the best" are yet and you end up interviewing more candidates than need be.

- Your interviews are far less effective. The test results give you the information you need to conduct an on-point, productive interview. You'll know where to focus your line of questioning so you get the most relevant information.

- You're setting yourself up for failure.

What happens if the applicant passes all the early tests and the interview and then fails the basic skill test for data entry speed? Or what if the true/false attitude test results show the applicant really does not want a job working with customers or dealing with paperwork? Up to this point, you and the applicant were both feeling it might be a pretty good match. What happens now?

You could say, "I'm sorry," to someone you thought you should hire. (Now, you're left to question your own judgment.) Or, you could rationalize and ignore the test results because you got such "good vibes" in the interview. (Now, you're taking an unnecessary risk.)

And then there's the applicant. This person has invested more time and pinned more hopes on this process than you have. Candidates rejected at this late point are understandably sorely disappointed and some may even challenge the test's validity. When you test early, the applicants who don't "pass" simply haven't done as well as other candidates – they didn't "fail" anything.

Selection System Tools

Types of Tests

***Get the applicants
to interview themselves.***

A variety of tests are available for assessing job-related capacities, attitudes, personality, and skills:

- **Capacities.** Tests can measure a person's ability to perform specific physical (lifting, bending, hearing, etc.) or mental (analytical, pragmatic, etc.) requirements of the job. When using a physical capacity test, be sure the applicant first signs a waiver releasing you from any liability. Only test for the ability to do the task and not the person's medical condition (pulse, blood pressure, etc.) during or after the test. Such qualitative tests are illegal.

- **Attitudes[7].** The main thing we're looking to hire is not skills, capacities, or personality; what we want are people with the right kinds of attitudes. Tests reveal attitudes by measuring an applicant's behavior, belief systems, and values in areas such as honesty, dependability, initiative, customer service, and safety orientation.

---

[7] See sample INSITE attitude evaluation on page 156 of the Tool Kit.

When a major convenience-store chain, with more than 600 stores across the country, gave its 1,000 customer service employees an attitude test, it found that nine percent said they would prefer a job where they didn't have to deal with customers. This would have been invaluable information to have up front – before any interviews. The company found out too late that 90 employees didn't really like dealing with customers.

- **Personality.** These tests provide an understanding of how the candidate's personality fits with the job, manager, and organization. These personality profiles measure traits such as competitiveness, relationship style, and attention to detail.[8]

The result of personality testing is like having six month's worth of experience with the person in just 20 minutes. A problem arises, however, when people use personality tests as the be-all, end-all. If the applicant's personality doesn't fit the job, the person isn't hired. You can lose good people if you only use personality evaluations. Remember, people are successful because they manage their personalities to get the job done effectively, whether they like doing a particular task or not. The real value of personality testing, therefore, is not to find the perfect match, but to identify areas to explore in the interview.

---

[8] See the OUTLOOK personality evaluation on page 161 of the Tool Kit section.

- **Skills.** These tests can measure an individual's level of proficiency in math, sales skills, supervisory skills, word processing skills, computer skills, etc. Every employer should always test for the skills that are essential to the successful performance of the job.

Selection System Tools

Test Validity

*Ask me a question and
I'll tell you no lie.*

When you see some of the true/false questions on attitude and personality tests, it may be difficult to imagine applicants being totally honest in their responses. Some typical true/false questions include:

- "If a friend asked for my employee discount, I would give it to him even though it was against the rules."
- "Everyone has shoplifted since becoming an adult."
- "I have stolen money from someone or some place in the last year."
- "Some of my close friends use illegal drugs."
- "I lose my temper easily."

Years of validity research prove that people do answer even these kinds of questions honestly and that their responses give an accurate picture of the individual's personality or attitudes. The reason is because few of us think we're all that different from everybody else. If you ask a group of adults how many of them have ever driven over the speed limit, just about all hands will be raised. We'll admit that we broke the law because we figure everyone else has done it too.

The same goes for other issues. Someone with close friends who use illegal drugs, for example, tends to think everybody has plenty of friends who use drugs too. And we know that 80% of people who answer this way either don't show up for drug testing or don't pass the drug test. Isn't this information worth having?

Selection System Tools

Drug Testing

If you're not drug testing and all your competitors are, where will all the drug users apply?

Drug testing is a necessity. Research shows that 18 to 22 percent of the workforce uses illegal substances on a regular basis, and that this usage costs U.S. businesses $6.5 billion a year in lost time alone. Other costs related to employee drug use include:

- Accidents
- Workers' compensation claims
- Theft

The best way to avoid these costs is not to hire the problem in the first place. Include drug testing in your hiring system. Depending on the company's resources and the type of job being offered, you may wish to drug test all applicants or only those you offer employment to.

Selection System Tools

The Reference Verification Form

Where there's a will,
there's a way.

Verification of an individual's past job performance is essential in the hiring process. It's important to verify the applicant has been accurate and truthful on the application blank and résumé. According to the Society for Human Resource Management, 20 to 25 percent of all résumés and applications contain *at least* one major discrepancy. If you don't check references and it turns out an employee's employment record has been falsified, you can be held accountable and at risk for a negligent hiring lawsuit.

Unfortunately, it's difficult to get much useful information from past employers. Lawyers have convinced them not to release any information other than employment dates and salary. But there is a tool that can help – the reference verification form[9]:

- This form requests basic information regarding past jobs and employers, and asks applicants to rate themselves as they think their previous supervisors would in different categories of performance and for qualities such as initiative, dependability, productivity, effort, cooperation, and overall performance.

---

[9] See sample Reference Verification form on page 165 of the Tool Kit.

- A separate form should be completed for each of the applicant's last three jobs or at least covering the last five years of work.

- When talking to references, ask them to confirm the ranking information the applicant provided. Make sure to fax over the signed waiver beforehand that shows the applicant says it's okay for you to get information from the reference.

- Experience shows that employers get useful responses and reliable answers 90% of the time when they use this tool. This is because you're asking references to confirm versus release information about the applicant.

A performance appraisal form is another tool that can be used for reference verification. If the applicant had a performance appraisal on the last job, ask about the ratings received, what they were based on, and how the applicant feels he or she could have ranked higher. When you talk to the reference, ask the person to verify the information the applicant provided. Even better, ask the applicant if they have a copy of that appraisal and, if they do, ask them to provide you with a copy, then call the reference (to make sure it has not been altered in any way).

Selection Systems Tools

Create Your Own Tests
Use your imagination.

If you take full advantage of the fact that everything you do in the hiring process is a test, you'll discover all kinds of tests for your applicants. And they won't cost you anything:

- One client gets double use out of a math skills test by adding special instructions on the bottom of the sheet: "Do not turn this page over." On the back, the answers are printed – four of them incorrectly. This company is testing for honesty and basic math skills in one, simple step.

- The manager of an office-supply store uses the long walk from the front of the store to his office in the back as a test. When applicants arrive for an interview, he has them follow while he walks as fast as he can to his office. Those who are more than five steps behind aren't hired – they don't move fast enough.

- When checker applicants arrive for an interview at a grocery store, they're instructed to observe the checkers on duty for 10 or 15 minutes. During the interview, the applicants are asked which checker they think is the best and why.

- Another store manager walks the aisles with an applicant, asking for comments on what's done right, what's wrong, and what the applicant would do differently.

- A delivery company gives applicants the wrong address and no phone number the first time they come to the office. If they still arrive on time, they pass the test.

- When an auto repair shop needs people, applicants are asked to put together a model car. When good detailers are needed, interviewers carefully examine how applicants apply the decals.

Selection System Benefits

What's In It for Me?

Ninety-nine percent of the people
involved in the hiring process hate it.

By making the hiring process organized, consistent, and successful, a selection system alleviates much of the aggravation typically associated with recruiting and hiring:

- **Incomplete information.** A selection system is specifically designed to provide the quantity and quality of information needed to make good decisions.

- **Lack of sources.** By building active – versus passive – recruiting into a selection system, there will be sufficient sources of applicants.

- **Don't know what's needed.** The whole purpose of a system is to define what's needed so you can get it.

- **First impression/friendship syndrome.** Hiring is not about making friends. We don't have to like the person; we have to hire the best person for the job. A system gives us the tools and procedures to do that.

- **We don't like to choose.** Most of us learned at a very young age that we don't like choosing people. Whether we were doing the choosing or waiting to be chosen for a team on the playground, it was an anxious and often disappointing experience. Selecting a

new employee is no different. Our decision
has a huge impact on other people's lives and
careers – both those we hire and don't hire.
Hiring decisions also affect our own careers
and the performance of our entire organization. A hiring system makes choosing less
unpleasant and stressful because it builds in
fairness and allows you to accurately predict
a person's suitability for the job. When
there's a good selection system in place, we
can feel better about our choices.

Some of the many other benefits of having a selection
system include:

- **Identifies good workers.** A system that uses
  all available and appropriate tools properly
  can accurately predict a person's abilities,
  attitudes, and willingness to work. A good
  system sets up hiring managers and supervisors for success, not failure.

- **More and better information.** You'll have
  more information than 90 percent of your
  competing employers do before making a
  hiring decision – and you haven't even interviewed yet. Every piece of information helps
  you do a better job in the hiring decisions
  you make.

- **Consistency.** By using the same methods to gather information about all applicants for a job, you're able to evaluate and compare candidates fairly and accurately.

- **Saves time.** You get all this information without having to spend much of your own time. All these tools – a good application form, telephone screening, pre-screening questions, testing, and a reference verification form – require more of the applicant's time than yours. Testing, which might take 15 minutes to one hour of the applicant's time, only takes about five to 10 minutes of yours.

- **Makes the job harder to get.** Because applicants have to work hard and invest more time, they have more respect for the job. Hiring tough also suggests that you take hiring seriously, creating a sense that yours must be a good place to work.

- **Saves money.** When you make better hiring decisions, you have lower turnover and a higher return-on-investment.

- **Reduces legal exposure.** You're less vulnerable to employment-related lawsuits because you treat everyone equally in the hiring process and have the documentation to prove it.

- **Builds your reputation as a Magnetic Company®.** A company that makes applicants feel they are treated fairly in the hiring process is a company people want to work for.

- **Better hiring decisions.** Most importantly, you'll make better hiring decisions, and dramatically increase your chances of hiring the right person for the job the first time.

The Interview

Overview

Never mind the applicant, how competent is the interviewer?

Finally, after a person passes all the preliminary tests and you've used your tools to gather as much information as possible, you're ready to interview. Are you prepared?

The applicant is. Remember, there's plenty of help out there for job seekers – books, audio and videotapes, seminars, workshops, trade and professional organizations, and government agencies. Most applicants have responses ready for every good question you think you have and are usually far better prepared than the interviewer.

Invest your time in interviewing wisely. Don't set yourself up for pat answers and shallow information. Get the meaningful, truthful information you need to make the best possible hiring decisions:

- Plan.
- Create the proper environment.
- Relax the candidate.
- Listen.
- React appropriately.
- Stay in control.
- Know how to sell your company and the position.
- Close the interview.

The Interview

Preparation

What you see in the interview is better than anything you'll ever see again.

People will always attempt to put their best foot forward in an interview. They tend to look as good as – or better than – they think they need to be to get the job. You have to remember what you see is not necessarily what you'll get.

Many will tell you what they want you to hear, not what you want to know. They'll present themselves, their skills, and background in the most positive light possible, stretching reality to fit the shoes they think they need to fill.

There are exceptions. Some applicants are worse in the interview than you'll ever see again. They're so nervous they aren't themselves, but most applicants prepare like it's opening night on Broadway, and the interview is their chance to win a Tony.

Failure to realize applicants are always on their best behavior in the interview can cause interviewers to fall into one of these traps:

- **Halo effect.** The applicant looks and sounds so good you assume everything about him or her is perfect. You don't bother to ask the tough questions.

- **Hunger factor.** You need a person so badly that you miss or excuse clues he or she gives, such as being late for the interview or not following your instructions to completely fill out the application. You also may listen only for what the applicant says, ignoring how it's said.
- **Gut feeling.** Don't hire on gut feeling. If your gut says there's something wrong, believe it; if your gut says everything is great, doubt it.

The Interview

Planning

One hour of planning saves three hours of work.

Planning for the interview begins with understanding your objectives. When you know what you want to find out, you can figure out the right way to ask about it.

- **Approach**
    1. Will the applicant be interviewed once or several times?
    2. Will there be more than one interviewer at any one interview?
    3. What will be asked or covered in each interview?

- **Environment**
    1. Determine where the interview will be held.
    2. Decide on the physical layout and seating arrangement.
    3. Establish what the content of the interview will be.
    4. Review the job's C.A.P.S. (Capacities, Attitudes, Personality, Skills) analysis to determine what you need to know and why.
    5. Determine the questions you need to ask to get this information.

6. Arrange the questions in a logical sequence.
7. Review all information gathered via tools so far to get an overall perspective of the applicant. Look for incomplete information or discrepancies, inconsistencies, potential weaknesses, and potential strengths.

The Interview

Planning

*You wouldn't build a house
without a plan.*

When you take the time to develop a good interviewing plan, it:

- Gives you confidence.
- Gives the candidate confidence because you're organized and the interview flows smoothly and makes sense.
- Relaxes the candidate.
- Gives you complete information; you don't forget to ask any questions.
- Provides consistent information, so that you can compare candidates accurately and fairly.
- Saves time.

The Interview

Positioning

Comfortable people will tell us almost anything. Uncomfortable people will tell us almost nothing at all.

Creating the proper environment – mentally and physically – means doing what you can to ensure the candidate relaxes. Only comfortable applicants will give you all the information you need to make a good decision:

- **Mental positioning**
  1. Be prepared.
  2. Be on time.
  3. Greet the applicant warmly and restate your name and title.
  4. In the applicant's presence, ask the receptionist to ensure you're not disturbed. This lets the applicant know you think the interview is important.
  5. Minimize distractions – no phone calls, interruptions, or piles of paperwork around.
  6. For the first few minutes, or as long as it takes, make small talk about something like the weather or traffic and offer the applicant coffee or a soft drink. A couple of minutes of neutral, give-and-take conversation up front will improve the quality of the entire interview.

- **Physical positioning**
  1. Whenever possible, avoid interviewing across a desk. It creates a formal barrier between you and the applicant that's not only stressful, but blocks you from seeing 80 percent of the applicant's body language. Ideally, you and the applicant should sit side-by-side or in full view of each other.
  2. Before the interview, try out the seat you'll offer the applicant to make sure it's comfortable.
  3. If it's a group interview, make sure seating arrangements and assignments are designed for maximum comfort.

The Interview

Maintaining Control

Ninety-five percent of all applicants
come prepared to tell you only what
they think you want to hear.

Another key to positioning an interview is to establish and maintain control.

The wrong way to start out is to explain all about the job and the organization. When you do this, you're setting the applicant up to simply feed back what you've already said you need when you ask questions about the applicant's skills and abilities.

Instead, put yourself in control. Describe the position and company briefly. Then tell the applicant you want to gather information by asking questions and that you will answer any questions the applicant may have after that.

This will give you 100% control and keep both you and the applicant on track. Should the applicant interrupt the process with a question, remind him or her that you'll answer questions later. This keeps things at your pace, not the applicant's.

The Interview

Getting the Truth

The most important thing to cover is your expectation regarding truth and honesty.

People have a propensity to meet our expectations. Make sure you inform the applicant that you expect the truth. When you do this, you change most applicants' mindset. Now, instead of telling you what they think you want to hear, they will tell you what you've said you want to hear – the truth. This will also make you feel more comfortable about asking questions we usually don't like to ask – like those about drug use and criminal records.

This type of statement gets excellent results:

> "I'm going to be very open and truthful with you about the job and our company and I hope you're going to be open and honest with me about yourself. It doesn't matter if you've ever resigned or been fired from a job, or had difficulty with a former boss. As long as you tell me, we can take it under consideration. But, if you don't tell me and we find a problem when we do our background checks and look into your history, I can't hire you. Do you understand what it is I want?"

Then wait for the applicant to say something like, "Of course, you want the truth." Once you get that confirmation, you're ready to start with the interview questions.

We've found that when you tell applicants you want them to be honest, 90 percent of the population will be more honest in the interview than they had planned to be. Ten percent may still lie to you, but that's why we do reference and background checks.

The Interview

Applications & Résumés

Never interview from the
résumé or application.

While résumés and applications are important tools for planning the interview, don't work from them during the interview:

- Asking questions directly from a résumé allows the applicant to control the interview. Because the résumé presents only what the applicant wants you to know, that's exactly what you'll be talking about. You won't get the information you need to determine if the individual is really suited to the job.

- Asking questions directly from a completed application also keeps you from getting potentially helpful information. It's amazing how often applicants give different dates, jobs, and other information when you're not prompting them with what's on their application. Remember, every step in the hiring process is a test. If information differs or the applicant can't remember, it's not necessarily a failure, but it may give you some insight you wouldn't have otherwise had. Maybe dates just aren't important to them – or maybe the person is hiding something.

The Interview

Listening

*God gave us two ears and
one mouth for a reason.*

The more the applicant talks and you listen, the more information and insight you'll gain. A good gauge is 80/20 – if you find yourself doing more than 20 percent of the talking, you won't learn as much as you otherwise could.

And listen actively – not only to what applicants are saying, but also for the meaning behind the words. This is conveyed through volume, tone, and emphasis. A softly whispered, "I love you," conveys a different meaning and feeling than a boldly declared, "I LOVE YOU!" or hesitantly phrased, "I love you?" Listen for the implications of these kinds of intonations.

In fact, how words are said – the vocal part of communications – is three times more important to meaning than the actual words used. Research shows that word choice communicates 7 to 11 percent of meaning, while intonation contributes 33 to 37 percent.

The Interview

Body Language

*Applicants mean what they're doing,
as well as what they're saying.*

Even more important to understanding the real message being communicated is body language – eye movement, hand gestures, facial expressions, posture, and leg movement all communicate information. Body language accounts for the remaining 52 to 60 percent of meaning:

- It tells you whether the applicant is relaxed at the beginning of the interview or not. If not, spend more time getting the applicant comfortable before you do anything else.

- While there may be some obvious signals – fidgeting or abrupt movements – you're not looking for individual things. What you're really looking for are patterns in the person's body language and changes in those patterns. For example, detecting the body language when the person is relaxed versus when responding to something more difficult.

- Be aware that some seemingly obvious signals may be invalid. In today's diverse population, for example, you may encounter people from cultures where it's *not* acceptable to look you straight in the eye.

- If you detect a change in body language that suggests something other than what the person is saying, probe further by saying, "I don't understand," or "You seem uncomfortable about this."
- Make sure you keep the applicant relaxed and get the information you want by showing interest and concern with *your* body language.

The Interview

Using Silence

*You don't learn anything
when you're talking.*

Most people abhor silence and become extremely un-comfortable during a thirty-second lapse in the conversation. Think about what happens if your car radio goes dead while you're driving. Most people start pushing buttons to find out what went wrong. We can't stand silence.

One of the most important techniques an interviewer can use is the power of silence. When the applicant responds with silence to a question, the normal reaction is for the interviewer to step in and re-phrase the question – or even suggest an answer. You don't have to fill the silence. Instead, simply say you realize it's a difficult question and tell the person to take as much time as needed to think about it. Then wait.

If a question has a reason to be asked, it has a reason to be answered.

The Interview

Reactions

Keeping the lines of communication open.

The applicant's responses to your questions will raise thoughts, opinions, questions, and concerns of your own. What you do with them determines how open and honest the communications climate remains:

- **Avoid evaluative feedback.** Be as noncommittal as possible in your responses to the applicant.

- **Take notes.** This gives you something to refer to later when evaluating the candidate, and it enables you to go back and probe further into things the applicant says during the interview.

- **Use a separate sheet of paper**. Don't take notes on the application or résumé.

- **Be aware of what you write down and when.** Don't write down anything negative the applicant tells you at the time you hear it. Keep this information in mind until the next positive thing the applicant says, and then record it. If the applicant tells you about being fired from their last job and you write it down as he or she is telling you, the applicant will be guarded and less spontaneous for the rest of the interview.

The Interview

Red Flags
Heed the signs.

Certain behaviors and reactions displayed during the interview indicate cause for concern when they occur in areas that are important to the job:

- Poor personal appearance.
- Lack of interest and enthusiasm.
- Overemphasis on money.
- Condemnation of past employers.
- Late for interview.
- Failure to express appreciation for interviewer's time.
- Asks no questions about the position.
- Vague response to questions.
- Overly aggressive, conceited, superiority, or know-it-all complex.
- Inability to express oneself clearly.
- Lack of planning for career.
- Lack of confidence and poise.
- Unwilling to start at the bottom; expects too much, too soon.
- Makes excuses; evasive, hedges on unfavorable factors in record.
- Lack of tact.
- Discourteous, ill-mannered.
- Lack of maturity.

- Indecision.
- Lethargic, lack of energy/vitality.
- Merely shopping around.
- Wants job only for a short time.
- No interest in company or industry.
- Cynical.
- Low moral standards.
- Lazy.
- Intolerant; expresses strong prejudices.
- Inability to take criticism.

The Interview

Biases

*I'm not prejudiced and
I hate people who are.*

We all have biases, whether we're aware of them or not. When we find out someone is from the same city we're from, we tend to instantly bond with that person – even though there are 1.5 million people living there.

Here are some common traps interviewers fall into unless they're aware:

- **Interviewer filtering.** Because of differing life experiences, our individual assumptions and interpretations lead to different conclusions about the same information. By using more than one interviewer, you'll avoid individual biases about what responses mean and how well the applicant matches the requirements.

- **Stereotyping.** Blondes are dumb; accountants are boring; teenagers are lazy. Believing such generalizations keeps interviewers from seeing the real person.

- **Mirror imaging.** We tend to immediately like and trust people who are like us – went to the same school, drive the same kind of car, shop at the same stores.

- **Physical appearance.** We also tend to like people who physically remind us of people we like – the same hair, eyes, mannerisms, or other characteristics.

- **Premature decision-making.** Most people decide whether or not they're going to hire someone in the first few seconds of meeting them. Don't let the first impression be the only impression. (Keep telling yourself that what you see is not necessarily what you'll get.)

- **Personal theories.** Some people put stake in popular beliefs about predictors of behavior like taking applicants to lunch to see if they taste their food before salting it. You won't learn anything about anyone's on-the-job attitudes or decision-making abilities this way – you'll only learn how much he or she likes salt.

The Interview

Types of Questions

It's not just what you ask,
but how you ask it.

Different types of questions provide different kinds of information. Use a variety of these to get the most complete picture of the applicant:

- **Closed-ended.** A closed question is one that can be answered with "yes," "no," or any one- or two-word answer. Its only function is to confirm or provide very basic information. For example, most questions asked in the pre-screening part of the process are closed, i.e., "Do you have reliable transportation?"

- **Open-ended.** These questions elicit extensive and complete responses which reveal the person's views, opinions, thoughts, and feelings. Open-ended questions are what you want to build the major part of your interviewing process around. Examples include:

  1. Describe the boss who got the best performance out of you.
  2. What kind of environment do you feel most comfortable working in?
  3. What was the most difficult problem you've ever had when dealing with a customer?

- **Alternative.** This is a great way to get specific information without loading the question so that it indicates the "right" answer. An alternative question poses two or three possibilities and asks the person to indicate a preference. Examples include:
  1. Would you prefer working for a boss who gives you broad responsibilities and little direction or one who gives very specific tasks and guidelines?
  2. Would you prefer flexible hours or a specific schedule?
- **Situational.** These questions ask how the person dealt with a particular situation. Example: "In a case where you had to deal with an angry customer, what caused the situation and how did you deal with it?" By asking about actual involvement in a situation – instead of how the person would handle a hypothetical one – you get a more valid answer.
- **Reversal.** If you want deeper insight into an applicant's thought processes, motivators, and drivers, reversal questions are quite powerful. Essentially, this is simply a matter of asking why the person asked you a particular question. It can be used in several ways:
  1. About 15 or 20 minutes into the interview say, "I've been asking you a lot of questions. If you could ask me one question, what would it be?" No matter what the applicant asks, say,

"Of all the questions you could have asked, why did you ask me that one?" In other words, the key issue is not the question asked, but why it was the most important thing the person could ask at that point.

2. During the time you give the applicant to ask questions, find out why they've asked each question, as often as seems comfortable, by saying, "That's a very interesting question. Why do you ask?"

3. When you bring an applicant back for a second or third interview, request a written list of at least four questions or concerns the person has about the job or organization. At the interview, instruct the applicant to rank them in order of importance and then ask why each was ranked as it was.

Interview questions should also cover all the different categories of information you need to determine the best candidate for the job:

- Capacities
- Attitudes
- Personality
- Skills
- Background
- References

The Interview

Keep It Legal

Certain questions set you up for legal problems.

The best way to avoid being accused of discrimination is to ask the same questions of *all* applicants and to never ask questions regarding:

- Race
- Religion
- National origin
- Marital status
- Age
- Disability
- Worker's comp
- Injury
- Any other category protected by law in your state

It's not necessarily illegal to ask these questions, but problems arise when applicants claim you used their answers to these questions to discriminate against them in your employment practices. So, it's best not to ask them at all. If you're uncertain about the legality of a certain question, ask yourself, "How is this information related to the job?" If it's not job-related, don't ask.

There's always a way, however, to obtain necessary information in a job-related and non-discriminatory manner:

- If you're concerned about marital status interfering with business travel, while you can't ask if an applicant's spouse would mind if he/she traveled a lot, you can ask if the applicant is willing to travel as often as the job requires.

- Rather than asking if an applicant is a U.S. citizen, ask if they have a legal right to work in this country.

- Instead of asking about religious background, ask if there's any reason the applicant would be unable to work on Saturday or Sunday as required by the job. If there's something job-related you really need to know, you can ask about it – without asking discriminatory questions.

The Interview

Tough Questions

*Everything you always wanted to know,
but were afraid to ask.*

If you're not using testing to cover these bases, force yourself to ask the questions most of us don't normally like to ask. They'll help you make better hiring decisions.

- **Drugs**
    1. What was your last company's attitude about drugs?
    2. When was the last time you used illegal drugs?
    3. What drugs have you used other than marijuana?
    4. Would you be willing to take a drug test?

- **Criminal Activity/Theft**
    1. Have you ever been convicted of a felony?
    2. When was the last time you had a problem with the authorities?
    3. What would you do if there was evidence your boss was stealing from the company?
    4. What is the most expensive thing you've ever taken from work?

5. If you've ever worked a cash drawer, did anyone ever tell you your drawer came up short? (If the answer is "no," the person is probably lying.)

- **Values**

    1. What would you do if you were given credit for something a co-worker actually did?

    2. Have you ever been fired or asked to resign?

- **Performance**

    1. Have you ever received special recognition at work?

    2. How do you know when you do a good job?

    3. When I talk to your previous supervisor, what will he or she say about your performance?

- **Dependability**

    1. How many times were you absent from work last year for reasons other than personal illness?

    2. Can you meet our attendance requirements?

    3. What would be a reason, other than personal illness, that you couldn't be at work every day?

    4. What was the latest you made it to work in the last six months? Why?

- **Safety**

    1. When was the last time you were involved in an accident at work?

    2. What was your last company's attitude about safety and how did you feel about it?

    3. What percent of the time you're in a car do you wear a seat belt?

The Interview

Structured Interviews

The most successful interviews are conversations, not inquisitions.

There are literally hundreds of questions you can ask applicants to get the information you need.

The key is building a list that's specific to the job you're trying to fill. Your list also needs to follow a logical sequence, starting with easier questions and flowing naturally from one area to another. Once you determine the questions to be asked when interviewing for a particular job, formalize the plan on paper. Your plan becomes your structured interview form – a most productive interviewing tool.

A structured interview[10] can take one of two basic approaches:

- List 10 to 20 individual questions, including several for each area – capacities, attitudes, personality, skills, background, and references.

- List three or four themes. Each theme probes one or more areas at once and has several follow-up questions that focus the interview in a particular direction depending on what information and insight is appropriate to the job.

---

[10] See sample Structured Interview Form on page 167 of the Tool Kit.

The Interview

Question Sets

*What we are now is
what we were then.*

A structured interview follows a certain theme throughout the interview. For example, one theme asks applicants to tell about their very first paying job and the three most important things learned in that job. Then you ask about the next job and the next, until you have a good overview of the person's entire work history.

In other words, it allows you to look at the person in a systematic way. It tells you a lot about the person's background and capacities, and also gives insight into personality and attitudes. What people learned at ages 15, 16, and 17, in their first jobs, they're usually still doing. If they learned to be dependable, they're dependable now. If they never got caught doing something they shouldn't, they're still probably doing it.

The first job question is a good opener because it's non-threatening, applicants usually aren't prepared for it, and you won't hear canned answers.

You can customize this theme to the position you're trying to fill by adding follow-up questions that target what you need.

If you need someone who can learn quickly and train others, ask applicants how they learned each previous job, if they ever trained anyone else to do that job and, if so, what are the most important things to do when training someone?

When you get to any job you're particularly interested in, you can always stop and ask more about it: "What did you like best about it?" "Why did you leave?" "If you could have changed one thing to make you stay there, what would it be?"

In today's diverse population, however, not every applicant's work history goes back to high-school age. While 90 percent of all high-school students raised in the U.S. have worked, there may be reasons an applicant never held a paying job during school. In some cultures, school is an absolute priority. Someone who excelled on a sports team probably devoted as much time, energy, and discipline to that as anyone does to a paying job.

So, don't immediately think not having a job while in school means the person is lazy or has a poor work ethic. The person may have had other responsibilities or interests that required hard work and dedication.

The Interview

Skill & Capacity Questions

When you ask about a person's weaknesses,
you get a weak answer.

Another theme centers around getting accurate information about an applicant's skills and capacities: "On a scale of one to 10, where 10 is perfect, how would you rank yourself as a cashier?" Ask this question about every skill and capacity the ideal candidate needs to have.

Follow-up questions probe further into each response, asking for details and examples of why applicants give themselves these ratings. Then ask what they think it would take for them to get the next higher rating.

For every skill or capacity that's essential to the job, this approach enables you to identify an applicant's level of competency, ability to adapt to the job, and do it effectively. It can be very revealing about what applicants can and want to do as long as you ask for this information before you tell people exactly what the job requires.

Consider, for example, the candidate who interviewed for an accountant's position. As a CPA, she ranked herself as a "9;" but in audit work, she only ranked herself a "2." If she had been told up front that the job required a lot of audit work, her response would have been different.

The use of this theme is much more effective than asking about an applicant's "weaknesses." Traditionally, questions about "weaknesses" get prepared responses that are more about strong points than areas needing improvement.

The Interview

Attitude & Personality Questions

Past performance is the best indicator of future performance.

Self-rankings can also provide insight into applicants' attitudes and personality traits. In this case, you ask them to rate their performance in various categories – initiative, dependability, quality, effort, job knowledge – as they think their former supervisors will rate them. With follow-up questions, ask why they think the boss will tell you the applicant rated as indicated and what would have been needed to receive a higher rating.

In other words, this is a way to use the reference verification form[11] for interviewing purposes as well as for background confirmation.

Another way to get this information is to ask applicants if they had a performance appraisal at their previous job. If they did, ask how they were evaluated for each skill and competency, and what it would take for them to do better.

---

[11]See sample Reference Verification Form on page 165 of the Tool Kit.

The Interview

Sell Them on the Company

First impressions are lasting.

Just as applicants want to sell you on their qualifications for the job, you have to sell them on the position and organization. Good workers want to join winning teams, so you need to give them good reasons to want to work for you. Remember, you only have one chance to make that first impression.

When the interview comes to the point where you explain the job and organization in more detail, cover the following:

- Rules.
- Expectations.
- Duties, responsibilities, skills, and attitudes required for the job.
- Positives about the job and organization.
- Negatives about the job and organization.

Just as you don't want applicants to lie to you, don't lie to them. Be honest about responsibilities as well as growth opportunities. If you're conning people to get them to come to work for you, it won't take long for them to figure it out – and pay you back!

The Interview

First-Time Workers
That first job is habit-forming.

When hiring first-time workers, employers have special challenges and responsibilities:

- **Recruiting.** To attract people looking for their first job, make sure your recruiting methods and messages convey that you're an upbeat, fun, flexible employer. At the same time, emphasize that you're looking for people who are responsible and dependable.

- **Interviewing.** Help calm their first-job jitters and compensate for their lack of work experience by doing whatever you can to get them relaxed. Tell them what you want in the way of answers – honesty, openness, and truthfulness. Possible questions to replace those about previous work experience include:
  1. Why do you want to work?
  2. Why do you want to work for this company/organization?
  3. Why should I hire you?
  4. How do you get your spending money now?
  5. What do you think it takes to be a good (job title)?
  6. Have you done anything before to earn money?

7. What five words would your friends use to describe you?

8. What five words would you use to describe yourself?

9. Have you ever had a problem learning something?

10. What are you proud of?

11. What's the worst trouble you've ever been in?

- **Training.** Once hired, you have an obligation to properly train them – not only in the job, but also in what it takes to be a good employee. The work habits and attitudes they learn with you will set their standards for the rest of their careers.

The Interview

Closing

End the interview as effectively
as you conduct the rest of it.

There's no reason to lose control at the very end of the interview, but it seems to be where most interviewers run into the problem. Keep things on track by closing with these three questions:

- Give applicants a chance to sell you on their interests and qualifications by asking: "What is the one reason I should hire you over anyone else to be a member of my team?"

- Then ask, "What is the one reason I shouldn't hire you?" At least 90 percent of the time, you'll get an answer that means absolutely nothing, but ten percent of the time you'll be really glad you asked. You'd be surprised how many people will volunteer something like they lose their temper easily, just had a back injury, or any number of things that may keep you from hiring a problem that you really didn't want to have.

- Finally, close with, "What else would you like to tell me about yourself that you haven't had a chance to tell me?" This ends the interview on a positive note.

Before applicants leave, also tell them what the next step is – for them to call you back, you'll call them, schedule another interview, take a drug test, etc.

The Interview

Evaluating the Applicants

Don't compare apples to oranges;
you'll just end up with fruit salad.

During the interview, an interview rating form[12] helps you rate the applicant in areas like communication skills, self-confidence, intelligence, ability to get along with others, and overall suitability for the position. Such a tool also provides a standardized, systemized approach when more than one person interviews a candidate and when evaluating one applicant against another.

Using the form as you talk to the candidate gives you a place to take notes and serves as a guide to make sure you cover all the required competencies and important points.

---

[12] See sample Interview Rating Form on page 170 of the Tool Kit.

The Interview

Making a Decision

*If your gut tells you not to
hire someone, don't.*

When making a final decision about whether or not to hire someone, there are four things to consider:

- Test results should count for 30 percent.
- The interview should count for 30 percent.
- References should count for 30 percent (if you're good at checking them).
- Your personal perception should count for only 10 percent.

No matter how hard you try to eliminate your biases – positive and negative – they may still be there. Recognize them and put them aside. Ask yourself, "How would I feel if this person went to work for my competition?"

If the applicant scores poorly in any one of these criteria, it's worth 100 percent and eliminates the applicant as a candidate. But a good rating in any one of these areas can't, on its own, get someone hired. It takes good ratings in all four.

The Interview

Tell Them Why

*Tell 'em why you'd hire 'em
and why you'd fire 'em.*

By spelling everything out up front, you avoid the mis-understandings, disappointments, and assumptions that can lead to having to fire someone:[13]

- **Why you'd hire the person.** Explain how the applicant's capacities, attitudes, personality traits, and skills are a good match for the job. In this way, you set expectations early. The person will either be able to meet your criteria or de-select themselves.

- **Job offer.** Make sure the person understands all the terms and conditions of the job offer – position, salary, starting date, any contingen-cies (such as a physical exam), and offer limits. At the hourly level, most employers cover this verbally, but there are advantages to putting the job offer in writing:

    1. It further ensures the person under-stands all terms and conditions.
    2. It communicates that the employee is a welcome addition to the organization.
    3. It makes applicants feel their arrival is important to the organization.
    4. It raises the image of your company a level above everyone else, helping es-

---

[13] See the Commitment Card on page 172 for a good example of one easy way to do this.

tablish its reputation as a *Magnetic Company®* – a place where people want to work.

- **Why you'd fire the person.** Make sure the person knows the grounds for termination by reviewing all job-related rules and your company's performance appraisal form. Verify that all new hires agree to abide by the rules, preferably by signing and dating a copy for their employment file.

The Interview

Notifying Unsuccessful Applicants

Being polite never hurt anyone.

Don't forget to notify the other candidates that you have made a decision to hire someone else, thank them for applying, and wish them well.[13] You don't want to create bad feelings in people who:

- May already be or could become customers.
- Who have friends and relatives who are or could be customers or business partners.
- Who you may want to hire at some time in the future.

---

[13] See a suggested letter on page 173 of the Tool Kit.

Tool Kit

We are an Equal Opportunity Employer. All applicants are considered without regard to race, color, religion, disability, sex, national origin, age (for those age 40 or over), or any other basis protected by federal, state, or local law. This employment application is only active for 30 days. After this time period a separate employment application must be submitted in order to be considered for employment.

PERSONAL

PLEASE PRINT CLEARLY   Date _____

First Name _____ Middle _____ Last _____

Street Address _____ Social Security No. _____

City/State/Zip _____ Phone (___) _____

How did you find out about this job?   ❑ Newspaper   ❑ Referral   ❑ Other _____

If hired, do you have a reliable means of transportation to get to work?   ❑ Yes   ❑ No   What is it? _____

Minimum salary expected _____ Are you at least 18 years old?   ❑ Yes   ❑ No

If the job you are applying for requires driving: Driver's License No. _____ State Issued _____ Expiration Date _____

Are you legally eligible for employment in the U.S.?   ❑ Yes   ❑ No (Proof of U.S. citizenship or immigration status will be required if hired.)

Have you been convicted of a felony in the last seven years?   ❑ Yes   ❑ No   Are you currently on parole?   ❑ Yes   ❑ No

Are you currently awaiting trial?   ❑ Yes   ❑ No   Are you currently on deferred adjudication?   ❑ Yes   ❑ No   If you answered yes to any of the previous questions, state the nature of the offense and disposition of the case. Include dates and places. (NOTE: Felony convictions or the existence of a criminal record do not constitute an automatic bar to employment.) _____

EMPLOYMENT DATA

Are you seeking: ❑ Temporary   ❑ Full-time   ❑ Part-time   What position(s) are you applying for? _____

What hours and shift(s) would you prefer to work? _____

What hours and shift(s) would you prefer not to work? _____

Please indicate any shift(s) you would not be available to work. _____

Are you willing to work overtime?   ❑ Yes   ❑ No   Weekends?   ❑ Yes   ❑ No   Holidays?   ❑ Yes   ❑ No

Are you currently employed?   ❑ Yes   ❑ No   If hired, when would you be able to start? _____

Have you ever worked for this organization before?   ❑ Yes   ❑ No   If yes, name used: _____

List any friends or relatives employed by this company: _____

Are you on layoff and subject to recall?   ❑ Yes   ❑ No

Have you ever been discharged or asked to resign from any position?   ❑ Yes   ❑ No   If yes, please describe: _____

How many days have you missed from school or work within the last year other than approved vacation, sick, or disability leave? _____

How many days have you been late to school or work within the last year other than approved vacation, sick, or disability leave? _____

Please describe: _____

If applicable, please refer to the attached job description for the position for which you are applying. Are you able to perform all these tasks with or without reasonable accommodation?   ❑ Yes   ❑ No Please describe which tasks, if any, you will need and accommodation to perform, and explain what type of accommodation you will need: _____

EDUCATION (Circle highest level attained.)

Elementary: 1   2   3   4   5   6   7   8   Secondary: 9   10   11   12   G.E.D   College: 1   2   3   4   5   6   7   8

Name of School: _____   Name of School: _____   Name of School: _____

Location of School: _____   Location of School: _____   Location of School: _____

If currently in high school, are you enrolled in a recognized co-op program?   ❑ Yes   ❑ No   Degree & Major: _____

If yes, identify program and school: _____   Minor: _____

MILITARY SERVICE

Are you a veteran?   ❑ Yes   ❑ No   If yes, give dates of service: From _____ To _____ List any special skills or training: _____

WORK HISTORY (Please list your last four employers. Begin with the most recent.)

1. Company _____ Phone No. with Area Code (_____) _____
   Address _____ City/State/Zip _____
   Dates of Employment: From _____ To _____ Salary: Beginning _____ Ending _____
   Job Title _____ Supervisor's Name & Title _____
   Describe duties briefly: _____
   Specific reason for leaving: _____

2. Company _____ Phone No. with Area Code (_____) _____
   Address _____ City/State/Zip _____
   Dates of Employment: From _____ To _____ Salary: Beginning _____ Ending _____
   Job Title _____ Supervisor's Name & Title _____
   Describe duties briefly: _____
   Specific reason for leaving: _____

3. Company _____ Phone No. with Area Code (_____) _____
   Address _____ City/State/Zip _____
   Dates of Employment: From _____ To _____ Salary: Beginning _____ Ending _____
   Job Title _____ Supervisor's Name & Title _____
   Describe duties briefly: _____
   Specific reason for leaving: _____

4. Company _____ Phone No. with Area Code (_____) _____
   Address _____ City/State/Zip _____
   Dates of Employment: From _____ To _____ Salary: Beginning _____ Ending _____
   Job Title _____ Supervisor's Name & Title _____
   Describe duties briefly: _____
   Specific reason for leaving: _____

May we contact all of the employers listed above? ☐ Yes ☐ No   If not, tell us which one(s) you do not wish us to contact and why. _____

How many jobs have you had in the last five years not listed above? _____

Why are you seeking a new position at this time? _____

List any business-related outside interests and organizations you're active in: _____

PLEASE READ THE FOLLOWING CARFULLY, THEN SIGN AND DATE THE APPLICATION.

Humetrics, Inc. • 8300 Bissonnet, Suite 490 • Houston, TX 77074 • 800-627-4473 or 713-771-4401 • Fax: 713-771-0501

Better Business Through Better Hiring℠

INSITE

PRE-EMPLOYMENT ATTITUDE EVALUATION
REVISION 2W

Company _____

Location _____

Last Name _____

First Name _____

Social Security Number ___ - ___ - _____

Position Applied For _____

EEOC COMPLIANCE NOTICE

Questions relating to race, sex, age, or national origin are asked in order to obtain information to demonstrate compliance with Federal and State regulations. They are in no way used in evaluation of this questionnaire. Supplying this information is **voluntary**. Employment decisions will not be made based on the information provided on this form. This information will be kept strictly confidential.

Sex:	**Date of Birth:**	**Ethnic Background:** (You may check more than one.)
❑ Male	___/___/___	❑ African-American ❑ Caucasian
❑ Female	MO. DAY YEAR	❑ American Indian/Alaskan Native ❑ Hispanic
		❑ Asian/Pacific Islander ❑ Other

PROFESSIONAL PARTICIPATION AGREEMENT

I will answer each question truthfully and to the best of my ability. **I understand any attempts to deceive or mislead will be detected and reported to the company.** I authorize Humetrics, Inc. to analyze this pre-employment evaluation and report the results to the company.

Signature _____

Date _____

*The following questions were developed to measure your personal style of thinking and acting. There are **no** right or wrong answers. Each person will answer the questions differently due to the differences between each of us as individuals. Read each statement and indicate whether it is TRUE or FALSE. If the statement is TRUE for you, circle T. If the statement is FALSE for you, circle F. You must answer **every** question.*

1.	I find it easy to talk to people.	T	F
2.	I am willing to work as hard as necessary to reach my goals.	T	F
3.	New cars are more expensive today than they were in the past.	T	F
4.	I lose my temper easily.	T	F
5.	I do not find these questions hard to read.	T	F
6.	I am one of the main leaders in every group I join.	T	F
7.	I am not sure where I want to be 5 years from now.	T	F
8.	I sometimes hurt other people's feelings without ever realizing it.	T	F
9.	Generally, I remain happy in spite of troubles.	T	F
10.	I have had a number of accidents in the last few years.	T	F
11.	When a customer is rude to me, it is okay to put them in their place or ignore them.	T	F
12.	Even when I was young, my friends looked to me as their leader.	T	F
13.	The best way to deal with a nasty customer is to avoid them.	T	F
14.	I work harder than most people.	T	F
15.	I would tell a fellow employee to stop if I knew he or she was stealing from work.	T	F
16.	I always seem to be running late.	T	F
17.	I am very optimistic about my future.	T	F
18.	Rules are important to running a good organization.	T	F
19.	When you work hard, things usually work out.	T	F
20.	Some of my friends think I am too uptight about some things.	T	F
21.	I have done something in the past that I was punished for.	T	F
22.	I could find a good reason to steal from work.	T	F
23.	I am usually friendly to everybody.	T	F
24.	I plan to stay on this job at least one year.	T	F
25.	My mood seems to change frequently.	T	F
26.	I would cancel an important social engagement if I were needed at work.	T	F
27.	I like helping people.	T	F
28.	If a friend asked for my employee discount, I would give it to him or her even though it was against the rules.	T	F
29.	I take longer than most to finish my work.	T	F
30.	I very seldom ask for help, even when it feels like I am in over my head.	T	F
31.	I have never lied to anyone.	T	F
32.	I tend to be a little clumsy.	T	F
33.	There are times when my future looks depressing.	T	F
34.	It takes a lot to make me angry.	T	F
35.	The motto, "The customer is always right," is more important today than ever before.	T	F

Insite
RESULTS

| Name (First, Last): | Sam Sample | | | Page: | 1 |
| Social Security #: | 587-04-7964 | | | | |

	Scale Score				
Scale	0	50	100		Result
Customer Service	******************				**100%**
Dependability	*****************				**85%**
Initiative	*****************				**85%**
Safety	*****************				**85%**
Validity	****************				**80%**
Values	***************				**75%**

Insite
SPECIAL CONSIDERATIONS

Name (First, Last):   Sam Sample
Social Security #:   587-04-7964

Question		Answer
14.	I work harder than most people.	False
21.	I have done something in the past I was punished for.	False
33.	There are times when my future looks depressing.	True
37.	Everyone steals more than minor office supplies from work.	True
49.	I have gotten some really rotten breaks in life.	True
55.	Stealing has become a way of life in this country.	True
58.	Employees would not steal if employers would pay a fair wage.	True
60.	When a person cuts in front of me in line, I usually do not say anything.	True
77.	I have had a couple of bosses or teachers who really did not like me.	True
87.	I have had a major clash with a former boss or teacher.	True
90.	I have been a little depressed lately.	True
101.	I never tried to cheat at games, even as a child.	True

Insite
SUGGESTED INTERVIEW QUESTIONS

Name (First, Last):	Sam Sample
Social Security #:	587-04-7964

Question

1. Describe a situation where a boss did not like you. How did you handle the situation? What happened?

2. Do you believe employee theft is ever justified? Why or why not?

3. On a scale of 1-10, with 10 = high, how would you rate your willingness to work?

4. Tell me about a job where people seemed to work harder than you did, at least in your boss's eyes.

5. Tell me about a time when things didn't go your way. Why didn't they? How did you deal with the situation? What would you differently if the situation came up again?

6. Tell me about a time you felt discouraged about your future. What did you do? What was the result?

7. Tell me about a time you had a major personality clash with a boss or teacher. What was the result?

8. Tell me about a time you just couldn't get along with a boss.

9. Tell me about a time you witnessed someone stealing something. What did you do?

Better Business Through Better Hiring

OUTLOOK

PERSONALITY PROFILE
REVISION 2W

_____   _____
Company   Location

_____   _____
Last Name   First Name

_____ - _____ - _____   _____
Social Security Number   Position Applied For

PROFESSIONAL PARTICIPATION AGREEMENT

I will answer each question truthfully and to the best of my ability. **I understand any attempts to deceive or mislead will be detected and reported to the company.** I authorize Humetrics, Inc. to analyze this pre-employment evaluation and report the results to the company.

_____   _____
Signature   Date

The following questions were developed to measure your personal style of thinking and acting. There are no right or wrong answers. Each person will answer the questions differently due to differences between each of us as individuals. Read each statement and indicate whether it is TRUE or FALSE for you. If it is TRUE for you, circle T. If it is FALSE for you, circle F. You must answer every question.

1.	I find it hard to meet people.	T	F
2.	I get tired fairly easily.	T	F
3.	If a prospect dislikes my product or me, I generally feel less worthwhile.	T	F
4.	I like to be around a lot of people most of the time.	T	F
5.	I never had crying spells when I was young.	T	F
6.	I try to keep my personal life separate from my business life.	T	F
7.	My friends consider me an easy-going person.	T	F
8.	I don't have a written set of goals and objectives.	T	F
9.	I sometimes put off things I really don't want to do, but need to get done.	T	F
10.	I usually won't try to convince others of my ideas, even if I know I am right.	T	F
11.	My personality hardly ever changes.	T	F
12.	I would rather talk to one person than talk to a lot of people.	T	F
13.	I like people who argue with me.	T	F
14.	I find it really hard to put off doing something I really want to do.	T	F
15.	I am uncomfortable as the center of attention in a group.	T	F
16.	I find it easy to take criticism without having my feelings hurt.	T	F
17.	I tend to over prepare for sales calls.	T	F
18.	I usually tell my friends when I think they are wrong.	T	F
19.	I sometimes take too long to make up my mind about things.	T	F
20.	I feel better when I can be alone most of the time.	T	F
21.	I always make it a point to compliment others.	T	F
22.	I care a lot whether I win or lose at games.	T	F
23.	I would rather have a lot of casual friends than just a few really close friends.	T	F
24.	I get really impatient with people who can't make up their minds.	T	F
25.	My friends would describe me as very outgoing.	T	F
26.	I seldom worry about my health.	T	F
27.	I never tried to cheat at games, even as a child.	T	F
28.	I have never missed a deadline.	T	F
29.	I don't set specific goals for myself on a regular basis.	T	F
30.	I have hurt other people's feelings without realizing it.	T	F
31.	I lose patience when I have to pay close attention to a lot of details.	T	F
32.	I get upset if I can't finish a job once I start it.	T	F
33.	I sometimes don't complete projects that I start.	T	F
34.	Whenever I am working with other people, I will usually try to show them up.	T	F
35.	When I do a job, I like to have time to follow-up on the details.	T	F
36.	I have answered all of these questions truthfully.	T	F
37.	I would prefer to leave the details of a job to someone else.	T	F
38.	I do not have trouble talking to people I have not met before.	T	F
39.	Every day I make a list of my priorities.	T	F
40.	I don't like people who get sidetracked easily.	T	F

Outlook
RESULTS

| Name (First, Last): | Sam Sample | Page: | 1 |
| Social Security #: | 000-00-0000 | | |

Scale	Scale Score			Result
	0	50	100	
Activity Cycle	**********			50%
Attention To Detail (2)	****************			80%
Call Inclination (2)	************			60%
Competitiveness	**************			70%
Dominance	********			40%
Emotional Awareness	****************			80%
Goal Setting	**************			70%
Impulsiveness	********			40%
Relationship Style	************			60%
Self Consciousness	************			60%
Sociability	**********			50%
Validity	****************			80%

Outlook
SPECIAL CONSIDERATIONS

Name (First, Last):   Sam Sample
Social Security #:   000-00-0000

Question		Answer
8.	I don't have a written set of goals and objectives.	True
27.	I never tried to cheat at games, even as a child.	True
34.	Whenever I am working with other people, I will usually try to show them up.	False
37.	I would prefer to leave the details of a job to someone else.	True
49.	I am more easily embarrassed than most people I know.	True
50.	I never feel worthless and no good.	False
61.	I hardly ever jump to conclusions without all the facts.	True
62.	I don't like to talk alot around people I don't know.	True
80.	I have done something in the past I was punished for.	False
90.	I like jobs that require a lot of detail.	False
109.	There are some people I just don't feel comfortable calling on.	True

REFERENCE VERIFICATION FORM

PLEASE PRINT

Applicant's First Name _____ Middle _____ Last _____

I give _____, the "Company", permission to obtain the employment references necessary to make a hiring decision and hold persons giving references free from any and all liability resulting from this process. I waive any provision impeding the release of this information and agree to provide any information necessary for the release of this information beyond that provided on the employment application and reference verification form.

_____   _____
Signature   Date

COMPANY INFORMATION

Company	Address	Phone	From Mo. & Yr.	To Mo. & Yr.
Job Title	Reason for leaving		Supervisor's Name and Title	
Describe duties briefly:			Starting Salary	Ending Salary

JOB INFORMATION

Did you work overtime? ❑ Yes ❑ No How often? _____

Were you ever counseled about attendance or tardiness? ❑ Yes ❑ No If yes, how often? _____

Did you have a performance review? ❑ Yes ❑ No What was your last performance review rating? _____

What comments did your supervisor make at that time? _____

REFERENCE INFORMATION

When we speak to your former supervisor, we will ask him or her to rate your performance with regard to the following categories. Please rate yourself in the following categories as you feel he/she will rate you:

TEAMWORK: The degree to which you are willing to work harmoniously with others; the extent to which you conform to the policies of management.

    Unsatisfactory   Below Average   Average   Above Average   Outstanding

DEPENDABILITY: The extent to which you can be depended upon to be available for work and do it properly; the degree to which you are reliable and trustworthy; the extent to which you are able to work scheduled days and times, as well as your willingness to work additional hours if needed.

    Unsatisfactory   Below Average   Average   Above Average   Outstanding

INITIATIVE: The degree to which you act independently in new situations; the extent to which you see what needs to be done and do it without being told; the degree to which you do your best to be a top employee.

    Unsatisfactory   Below Average   Average   Above Average   Outstanding

QUALITY: The degree to which your work is free from errors and mistakes; the extent to which your work is accurate; the quality of your work in general.

    Unsatisfactory   Below Average   Average   Above Average   Outstanding

CUSTOMER SERVICE: The degree to which you relate to the customer's needs and/or concerns.

    Unsatisfactory   Below Average   Average   Above Average   Outstanding

OVERALL PERFORMANCE: The degree to which your previous employer was satisfied with your efforts and achievements, as well as your eligibility for rehire.

    Unsatisfactory   Below Average   Average   Above Average   Outstanding

Did you resign from this position? ❑ Yes ❑ No Discharged? ❑ Yes ❑ No Laid-Off? ❑ Yes ❑ No

Were you ever disciplined on the job? ❑ Yes ❑ No Explain: _____

TELEPHONE REFERENCE VERIFICATION

APPLICANT INFORMATION

Applicant: _____ Date: _____

Supervisor's Name: _____ Title: _____

Company: _____City/State: _____ Phone (___) _____

SCRIPT

I would like to verify some of the information given to us by _____

who is applying for employment with our company. I have a signed release and authorization holding any persons giving references free from any and all liability that could result from this process.

REFERENCE INFORMATION

Please rate the applicant's performance with regard to the following categories:

TEAMWORK: The degree to which the employee was willing to work harmoniously with others; the extent to which he or she conformed to the policies of management.

| Unsatisfactory | Below Average | Average | Above Average | Outstanding |

DEPENDABILITY: The extent to which the employee could be depended upon to be available for work and do it properly; the degree to which he or she was reliable and trustworthy; the extent to which the employee was able to work scheduled days and times, as well as his or her willingness to work additional hours if needed.

| Unsatisfactory | Below Average | Average | Above Average | Outstanding |

INITIATIVE: The degree to which the employee acted independently in new situations; the extent to which he or she saw what needed to be done and did it without being told; the degree to which the employee did his or her best to be a top employee.

| Unsatisfactory | Below Average | Average | Above Average | Outstanding |

QUALITY: The degree to which the employee's work was free from errors and mistakes; the extent to which his or her work was accurate; the quality of the employee's work in general.

| Unsatisfactory | Below Average | Average | Above Average | Outstanding |

CUSTOMER SERVICE: The degree to which the employee related to the customer's needs and/or concerns.

| Unsatisfactory | Below Average | Average | Above Average | Outstanding |

OVERALL PERFORMANCE: The degree to which you were satisfied with the employee's efforts and achievements, as well as his or her eligibility for rehire.

| Unsatisfactory | Below Average | Average | Above Average | Outstanding |

Why did this employee leave your company? _____

Would you re-employ him or her? ❑ Yes ❑ No If no, why not? _____

Is there anything else we should know about this person? _____

What were the dates of his/her employment with you? From: _____ To: _____ What were his or her earnings? _____

HOW WOULD YOU DESCRIBE HIS OR HER:

Consideration for company property? _____

Dependability on completing assignments? _____

Supervision requirements? _____

Attendance? _____

Strengths & Limitations? _____

Job performance? _____

Additional comments: _____

To order, call Humetrics, Inc. ◆ 8300 Bissonnet, Suite 490 ◆ Houston, TX 77074 ◆ 800-627-4473 ◆ 713-771-4401

This form is sold for general use throughout the United States. Because state regulations change frequently, Humetrics cannot assume responsibility for the use of said form. Please call Humetrics and check with legal counsel regularly to ensure compliance within your state.

Applicant's Name _____ Position _____

Interviewer's Name _____ Date _____

*You may write on this form; **DO NOT** write on the application blank!*

REMEMBER: *It is illegal to ask any question that does not pertain to the applicant's ability to perform the job.*

CHECKLIST:

- ❏ Is the application complete?
- ❏ Are you and the applicant positioned correctly?
- ❏ Have you reviewed the steps of the interviewing process?
- ❏ Have you encouraged the applicant to be honest?
- ❏ Have you "sold" your company?

VERIFY KEY QUESTIONS: (*"I know these questions were on the application, but I want to review them with you."*)

NOTE: *As you are asking these questions, it helps to take notes. (Be careful to write down both the positive and negative statements.) Also, limit your comments and reactions to what they are saying.*

Look for individuals who are non-communicative in the interview or are evasive and vague in their answers to questions. Dishonest applicants tend to ride the fence and will often try to not express opinions until they feel confident they know the answer you want to hear.

1. Why are you looking for a job at this time?

    _____

2. How far away do you live from this job? Are you willing to work at another location?

    _____

3. Do you have reliable transportation? What is it?

    _____

4. What hours do you prefer to work? What hours are you available to work? What hours can't you work?

    Prefer: _____

    Available: _____

    Unavailable: _____

5. Have you ever been fired or asked to resign from a job? Explain.

    _____

    _____

*If the applicant is unwilling to work the hours you need or has other problems meeting basic criteria, diplomatically close the interview by telling him or her that the most qualified applicants will be contacted. **Do not make this a negative interviewing experience for the applicant!***

The interview is your chance to sell your company as a great place to work. Building rapport with employees begins here, with the applicant's first impression of the company closely matching his or her first impression of you, the interviewer. At the same time, you are making decisions concerning your company's most valuable asset – its people. For these reasons, it is important to continually improve your interviewing skills.

NOTE: *Begin the structured interview by building rapport with the applicant, making him or her feel comfortable. Then give the applicant a verbal outline of the conversation about to take place. The following is a sample of the type of introductory conversation you might want to use:*

I am so glad you decided to come in and apply. I want you to realize there are no right or wrong answers in this interview. So just relax and try not to worry about perfect answers. The only perfect answers are the ones you truly believe when you say them.

Here's what we are going to do. First, I would like to gather some information so I can get to know you a little better. Then, after my questions, I will give you some background on our company and the position in more detail. Finally, I will answer, to the best of my ability, whatever questions you might have. The most important thing you can do is be completely honest. Everyone has made mistakes. As long as you are honest about them, we will consider you for this position. If you aren't honest, however, and I find out, I can't hire you. And, if we do hire you, and information emerges indicating a lack of complete honesty, we will have to fire you. Therefore, complete openness and honesty are priorities here.

1. What do you think it takes to be a good _____?
   (Fill the blank with the job you're trying to fill, i.e., cashier, stocker, server, etc.)
   _____
   _____

2. How do you think you fit into this description and why?
   _____
   _____

3. Tell me about your first paying job. Tell me three things you learned in that job. Did you do anything before that to earn money? What was your next job? (Briefly review all jobs.)
   _____
   _____

4. Of all of these jobs, which did you enjoy the most? Why? The least? Why?
   Most: _____
   Least: _____

5. Of all of these jobs, which was the hardest? Why? How long were you at this job?
   _____
   _____

6. Tell me about the best boss you ever had.
   _____
   _____

7. Describe the worst boss you ever had.
   _____
   _____

8. Have you ever been fired or asked to resign from a job, and if so, what were the circumstances?

_____

_____

9. How many days did you miss work in the past year due to something other than personal illness? Why?

_____

_____

10. Did you stay late or come into work early on short notice in your last job? Could you do so in this one?

_____

_____

11. Have you ever been in a cash handling position before? What was the largest amount your drawer ever came up short? How was this issue resolved?

_____

_____

12. Tell me about a time you dealt with a difficult customer, co-worker, supervisor *(choose the most appropriate)*. How did you handle that situation?

_____

_____

13. How often do you play lottery, video poker, or scratch-off game cards?

_____

_____

14. What illegal drugs have you used?

_____

_____

15. Is there anything else you would like to tell me?

_____

_____

_____

_____

Applicant's Name _____   Position Interviewed For _____

INSTRUCTIONS: Rate the applicant on his or her suitability for the position for which he or she is applying. To help you, nine traits are listed below to assist you in arriving at a rating. These traits are not meant to be all inclusive, but are presented to assist you in arriving at a numerical rating. The statements under each trait are, again, an aid in determining a rating. Your final rating of the candidate will be shown in *Item 9 - Suitability for this Position*. Should you determine additional traits apply to your organization's needs, space is provided for recording these impressions under *General Comments*.

1. **APPEARANCE:** Consider the applicant's personal appearance, bearing in mind the requirements of the position. Does he or she present a satisfactory appearance as a representative of the company? *Observe: dress, neatness, posture, sitting position, facial expressions, mannerisms.*

1 2 3	4 5 6	7 8 9	10 11 12	13 14 15
Unacceptable	Unsatisfactory	Acceptable w/reservations	Acceptable	Outstanding

2. **PHYSICAL CAPACITY:** Consider the essential job functions and the applicant's physical ability to perform the duties of the position with or without accommodation. If the position requires heaving lifting or bending, does he or she possess the physical strength to do so?

1 2 3	4 5 6	7 8 9	10 11 12	13 14 15
Unacceptable	Unsatisfactory	Acceptable w/reservations	Acceptable	Outstanding

3. **ABILITY TO GET ALONG WITH PEOPLE:** Consider the applicant's attitude toward the interviewer. Does he or she appear to be friendly, polite, and likable? Does the applicant command respect? Is he or she over-sensitive to criticism? Is there antagonism, indifference, or a cooperative attitude?

1 2 3	4 5 6	7 8 9	10 11 12	13 14 15
Unacceptable	Unsatisfactory	Acceptable w/reservations	Acceptable	Outstanding

4. **COMMUNICATION SKILLS:** Consider the applicant's choice of words, sentences, phrases and use of slang. *Observe: use of simple and correct grammar, hesitations, needless repetitions, technical word usage, logical presentation, coherence of thoughts.*

1 2 3	4 5 6	7 8 9	10 11 12	13 14 15
Unacceptable	Unsatisfactory	Acceptable w/reservations	Acceptable	Outstanding

5. **SELF-CONFIDENCE:** Consider the applicant's self-confidence. Is he or she nervous and ill-at-ease or poised and relaxed? Does the applicant appear to be uncertain or hesitant about his or her ideas? *Observe: embarrassment, stammering, tension, poise, hesitation, lack of confidence, over-confidence.*

1 2 3	4 5 6	7 8 9	10 11 12	13 14 15
Unacceptable	Unsatisfactory	Acceptable w/reservations	Acceptable	Outstanding

6. **INTELLIGENCE:** Consider the applicant's external demonstration of intelligence. Does he or she appear to grasp concepts easily? Is he or she a good listener? Does the applicant ask thoughtful and intelligent questions?

1 2 3	4 5 6	7 8 9	10 11 12	13 14 15
Unacceptable	Unsatisfactory	Acceptable w/reservations	Acceptable	Outstanding

7. **EXPERIENCE/JOB KNOWLEDGE:** Consider the applicant's work history. Does he or she have the minimum experience required for the job? Is he or she familiar with the techniques, processes, procedures, products, equipment, and materials required to do the job?

1 2 3	4 5 6	7 8 9	10 11 12	13 14 15
Unacceptable	Unsatisfactory	Acceptable w/reservations	Acceptable	Outstanding

8. **AMBITION:** Consider the applicant's motivation level. Does he or she appear eager to get the job and motivated to succeed? Although the applicant may be "qualified" for the job, is this a job that will really interest him or her, or is he or she just looking for anything?

1 2 3	4 5 6	7 8 9	10 11 12	13 14 15
Unacceptable	Unsatisfactory	Acceptable w/reservations	Acceptable	Outstanding

9. **SUITABILITY FOR THIS POSITION:** Consider the applicant's potential for success. Does he or she reply readily to questions asked? Are his or her ideas original? Are the applicant's statements convincing and appropriate? Is there evidence of leadership? Does he or she speak out voluntarily at proper times? Does the applicant have a definite interest in this work? Is he or she too eager for promotion? *Observe: alertness, responsiveness, tact, cooperation, enthusiasm.*

1 2 3	4 5 6	7 8 9	10 11 12	13 14 15
Unacceptable	Unsatisfactory	Acceptable w/reservations	Acceptable	Outstanding

GENERAL COMMENTS: _____

_____

_____

_____

SIGNATURE OF INTERVIEWER _____ DATE _____

TOTAL SCORE _____ OUT OF 135

To order, call Humetrics, Inc. ◆ 8300 Bissonnet, Suite 490 ◆ Houston, TX 77074 ◆ 800-627-4473 ◆ 713-771-4401

A PERSONAL COMMITMENT TO MY EMPLOYER AND MYSELF

INTEGRITY: The ability to make a promise and keep it.

By agreeing to the following commitments, I am giving my personal promise to uphold these standards:

❑ I promise to treat every customer and co-worker as I wish to be treated, with the utmost respect and courtesy.

❑ I promise to promote goodwill to all customers and co-workers and to handle customer concerns personally with the attitude that *"the customer is always right."*

❑ I promise to practice productive job behavior, arrive at work on time, and follow all rules, even when unsupervised.

❑ I promise to do what needs to be done to the best of my ability.

❑ I promise to uphold the standards and ethics the company has set for all its employees in regard to respect for property and the use of illegal substances.

❑ I promise to follow and actively promote all safety rules and regulations.

❑ I promise to uphold the company image in regard to my personal grooming habits, dress, and language.

My signature is as good as my word.

_____   _____
Employee's signature/date   Supervisor's signature/date

Suggested Letter to Unsuccessful Applicants

Dear _____:

Thank you for applying for a position with (company name). We appreciate the time and effort it took.

While we don't have any openings that match your skills, interests, and abilities at this time, if you would like to reapply at some time in the future, we would be glad to reconsider your qualifications.

Thank you again for thinking of (company name) as a potential employer.

We wish you all the best.

Sincerely,

Key Concepts

Index

About the Hire Tough Group

The Hire Tough Group is dedicated to helping our clients improve their process for recruiting, selecting, and retaining the best hourly employees. Our parent company, Humetrics, Inc., was founded over 20 years ago as a human resource consulting firm and offered our clients a wide range of solutions to their human resource needs. Over the past ten years, we have expanded our expertise and narrowed our focus by creating the Hire Tough Group to:

- Deliver keynote, general session, and breakout educational presentations as well as training workshops on the most efficient, cost-effective ways to recruit, select, and retain the kinds of quality hourly employees who will stay longer and be more productive.

- Undertake consulting projects including, but not limited to, recruiting and selection system audits, selection system design, and validation studies.

- Provide screening tools (employment forms and structured interviews) that give our clients a competitive edge when it comes to hiring the best hourly employees.

- Provide educational materials including a monthly newsletter, audiotapes, books, and manuals.

For more information, call 1-877-447-3868, or visit us on the web at http://www.hiretough.com.